MW00632708

URBAN INGREDIENTS

THE BEERS, STORIES & FLAVORS OF
GOOSE ISLAND BEER COMPANY

GOOSE UNIVERSITY PRESS

Published by
Raymond Press
An imprint of Prospect Park Books
www.prospectparkbooks.com

Library of Congress Cataloging in Publication data is on file with the Library of Congress
ISBN 978-1-945551-22-2

Text and recipes by Jenn Garbee

Edited by Christina Perozzi

The following photos are by Staci Valentine:
front cover, pages 44, 164, 178-179, 181, 184-185,
186-187, 188, 191, 192, 195, 198-199, 200-201, 202, 207, 208,
210-211, 213, 216, 219, 220, 223, 226-227, endpapers.

The following photos are used by permission of Getty Images:
pages 61, 77, 148, 151, 172, 173, 183, 196-197.

All other photos property of Goose Island Beer Company; most were taken by
staff photographers Ken Hunnemeder, Mike Erickson, and Ryan Grillaert.

Design by Lentini Design & Marketing, Inc.

Printed at Versa Press in Illinois, USA

INTRODUCTION 7

THE STORY 8

The Goose Island Story 10

Elk Mountain Farms 34

Goose Lessons 42

THE BEER 54

Brewing 101 56

Our Beers 80

THE FLAVORS 144

Tasting, Storing & Serving Beer 146

Beer & Food Pairing 174

RECIPES 198

Brewer's Waffles 202

Beer Cocktails 204
Sofie-Mosa
Fleur de Saison
Pimm's IPA
Urban Ginger
C.A.L.M. Daiquiri
Matilda Spiked Cider
Matilda Apple Toddy

Bulgogi Breakfast Tacos 206

Herb-Cured Gravlax 208

Sicilian-Style Citrus Salad 210

Chicken Shio Ramen 212

Condiments 216
Balsamic Nut Relish
Red Onion Stout Marmalade
Apricot Ginger Chutney
Habanero Carrot Hot Sauce

Scallops with Arugula & Beurre Blanc 218

Lamb Korma 220

Bourbon "Bread Pudding" Ice Cream 222

Barley Brown Butter Sand Tarts 225

ACKNOWLEDGMENTS 228

PHOTO CREDITS 229

INDEX 230

INTRODUCTION

Making friends for the brewery:

that's our mission here at the Goose Island Beer Company. To do that, we need to consistently brew delicious and imaginative beers. That's where it starts, but a brewery needs to have a personality and a soul as well. This is what our founder, John Hall, dreamed of and built at the original brewpub on Clybourn Avenue, and it has remained a bedrock of our success to this day. Anyone who visited the brewpub since it opened in 1988 was likely to be warmly welcomed by John and asked, "What'll it be?"

Making friends for the brewery also means being generous and committed to our city by bringing people together for worthwhile causes. Through the years, Goose Island has supported countless charitable organizations with donations, fundraisers, and sponsorships, and we've had a load of fun doing it.

That personality and soul is internally focused as well. It is revealed in the reverence that Goose Island employees have for the craftsmanship and beauty of a well-brewed beer. It's also revealed by the high level of camaraderie shared among our staff, whether we're having a pint in the taproom or navigating the rigors of a challenging and demanding project. It would be impossible to make friends for the brewery if we weren't friends with each other first!

My personal memories of Goose Island go all the way back to the original days. The same year the brewery opened, I met my wife of almost twenty-two years. She happened to live on Sheffield Avenue, just around the corner from the brewpub. Some of our first dates were there, enjoying Honkers Ale and Lincoln Park Lager together. No wonder Goose Island has always held a special place in my heart.

This wonderful book is composed of many parts. You'll find the stories interesting, whether they are about the history of brewing in the city of Chicago or anecdotes from former Goose Island employees about their time here. The descriptions of the ingredients that constitute a great beer recipe and the information on the brewing process are educational and enjoyable. We also give you a peek into the renowned Goose Island barrel-aging program and warehouse, where we continue to create beers that garner a global following. That, and much more, is in store for you between the covers of this book.

In short, we're looking to make a few more friends for the brewery via this publication. So sit back, pour yourself a delicious beer (preferably a Goose Island), and enjoy.

Welcome to Goose Island! What'll it be?

Ken Stout
President
Goose Island Beer Company

THE
STORY

THE GOOSE ISLAND STORY

Curiosity Is a Powerful Force

It all began with a thunderstorm.

Goose Island Beer Company founder John Hall was just another business traveler stranded in an airport far from home. Departure screens promised flight delays, and smartphone distractions were still decades away. These are the moments that call for something to read, and if you're lucky, a good beer.

So John settled in for the long haul, pulled out a frequent flier airline magazine stashed in his carry-on from the last flight, and found an article about boutique beers from a few small American breweries that he thought was very interesting: "We didn't have anything like them in Chicago."

It's easy to take today's grassroots, local startup–friendly culture for granted. In the mid-'80s, a forty-something family man with a solid corporate job ditching everything to start a brewery? Hurry up and call a therapist already. Building a

business from scratch when you know a lot about business but virtually nothing about that particular business? (Other than sure, you really enjoy a good beer.) Good luck impressing bank loan officers.

"I had this romanticized vision of starting a brewery in Chicago," continues John. "All I knew was that I wanted to make the best beer that we could." A trip to England a few years earlier had fueled that passion, when John discovered flavors in beers—especially ales—that he had never tasted. Other than in a few craft beer–friendly pockets, back home "light" lagers low on flavor were still the norm. If John wanted to enjoy a richly flavored, English pub–style ale like Honkers Ale, he was going to have to make it. "Today, I still really appreciate a well-balanced, sessionable ale."

John never imagined that nearly three decades later, the brewery he founded would be respected as one of the most creative in the country, or that Goose Island Beer Company beers would be racking up frequent flyer miles of their own on international flight menus.

CHICAGO: CITY OF BROAD SHOULDERS

In 1988, the same year Goose Island Beer Company was founded, the Cubs played their first outdoor night game at Wrigley Stadium. It rained. Even in a city that waves the W flag high, life—and baseball—goes on. This story is as much about Chicago as it is about the first brewery to operate in the city for decades.

Chicago is a relatively young city in American history. By the early 1820s, only a handful of settlers, including Archibald Clybourn (see page 16), had migrated to the city. That would soon change. Chicago has an indescribable allure, the sort of "town" immortalized by Sinatra albums and tales of Hollywood-worthy gangsters. But work, plain and simple, was the original draw. Hard work and hard-earned respect: Chicagoans likely agree on little else and tell you as much. They have long worn their struggles and differences with pride.

Immigrants arrived by the hundreds of thousands as the city became the American hub for Midwestern staples like grain and beef; railcar and other manufacturing plants were booming. The Great Fire of 1871 nearly ended it all. Chicagoans rebuilt their lives, businesses, and the city from scratch. Again. They pulled out their best moussakas, pierogies, and Chinese dumplings to share at burgeoning restaurants. They met for drinks in local taverns stocked by local breweries. They worked hard.

By the early 1900s, the city was back on the map as the Midwestern business center. There is much more to tell, but we need to get back to beer.

MY KIND OF TOWN

The city's first commercial brewery opened in 1833, with a production run of about six hundred barrels of ale that first year. Pilsner would make an appearance about ten years later, when the first brewery serving the German-style lagers opened its doors. The brewing industry was right at home in a city like Chicago, where German immigrants served as knowledgeable Braumeisters, or brewers, and neighboring Midwestern farmers conveniently grew plenty of grain. The city was also situated alongside a famously vast expanse of fresh water. (Other than the polar ice caps, the Great Lakes are the largest system of fresh water on the planet.) As in other American cities, liquor was also very popular, although by the late 1800s, most Chicago distillers had moved their operations to other cities.

By the early 1900s, the city was brimming with more than fifty local breweries. Taverns and saloons served as gathering spots, and brewers opened their own beer bars. (Change the name to brewpubs, throw in a few social media posts, and it sounds remarkably familiar.) After a long day at work, local beers—and places to relax and enjoy them— were plentiful. We all know what happened next: everything would come to a screeching halt. Gangsters couldn't believe their good luck.

> ## "IT'S EASY TO FORGET
> ## TODAY *that John built this company out of nothing when no one really did that. He had a vision that the beer industry was going to be different, that beer was going to really change."*
>
> —John Laffler, former Goose Island brewer
> Founder and brewmaster
> Off Color Brewing, Chicago

As in other American cities, Prohibition left a mark on Chicago's drink industry even decades after the law was repealed. The few local breweries that reopened faced the challenges of a new beer era. Taverns and other brewpub-like gathering places were largely replaced by America's new "to-go" culture, fueled in part by the accessibility of the home refrigerator and the increasing popularity of aluminum cans and glass bottles. Food and beverages like beer could be shipped to and from any major city with access to railcars. Beginning in the '50s, the creation of interstate highways (a decades-long project) would pave the way for nationwide access to packaged food and drinks. Chicago became a major manufacturer of foods like confections (see Candyland, page 191) and sports drinks, but US beer production shifted to other major metropolitan areas.

When its doors opened in 1988, Goose Island Beer Company was the only local brewery in Chicago, and the city's first brewpub in decades.

John
HALL

FAVORITE BEER "I usually tell people that I appreciate any good beer style, or whatever beer I'm drinking right now. But I have always appreciated a sessionable (lower-alcohol) ale, maybe even more these days. I like both the style and that I can enjoy more than one."

One of John's favorite beers today is still the flagship Honkers Ale, a classically balanced and sessionable English-style pub ale.

BREWING ALLY "My wife, Patricia. She was the one person who didn't think it was crazy that a man in his forties with a good job wanted to start over and brew beer. Everyone else, from work colleagues to family, thought I was making a bad decision. She supported me through the entire process."

Patricia Hall came up with the name for Honkers Ale, Goose Island's flagship beer.

BIGGEST HURDLE "I didn't anticipate how difficult it would be to get people to even taste a different style of beer [ales and full-flavored lagers] back when light lagers dominated the national market. And here Goose Island is making lagers again. I love a good, crisp lager. To come full circle is the beauty of a great beer program."

The five inaugural beers offered on tap at Clybourn in 1988 were all full-flavored styles—including both lagers (Golden Goose and Lincoln Park):

Honkers Ale, Golden Goose Pilsner, Lincoln Park Lager, Old Clybourn Porter, and Honest Stout. (Honkers Ale remains a permanent fixture today; some of the others make special appearances.) Four Star Pils, released in 2015, was the first pilsner that Goose Island brewed and bottled on a national scale (a handful of earlier pilsners like Goose Pils were brewed in very limited quantities).

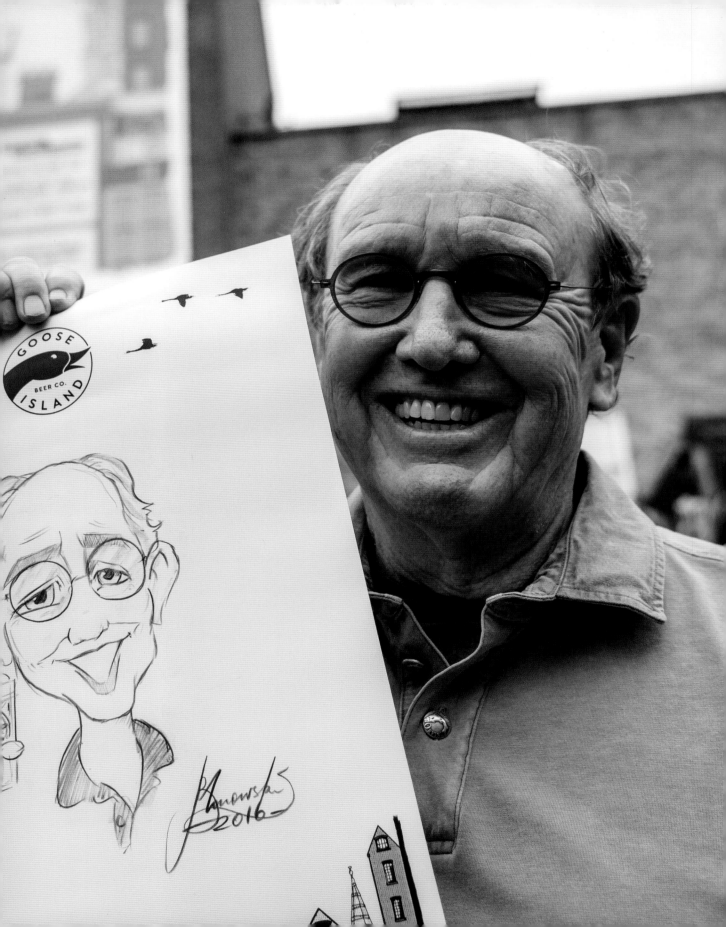

ROOTS IN THE HEART
OF THE CITY

"I thought I really knew Chicago, but when I started looking for a place, I realized I had a lot to learn," recalls Goose Island Beer Company founder John Hall. "Wanting to really get to know the heart of the city for the first time led me to Clybourn Avenue."

The name Clybourn is one of Chicago's oldest. When Virginia native Archibald Clybourn and his family arrived in Chicago in the early 1820s, only a few dozen settlers lived in the fledgling city. (The area was primarily inhabited by Native Americans.) While still in his twenties, Clybourn built Chicago's first large-scale slaughterhouse, the source of his vast wealth and the precursor to the city's massive stockyards. He later served as the city's first constable, on the school board, and in other influential positions. Wealth, power, and politics tend to breed controversy, and Clybourn was no exception. But his mark on Chicago is an indelible stamp that contributed to the city that we know today.

1800 North Clybourn Avenue

Today, the Lincoln Park neighborhood on Chicago's North Side is the sort of urban center where converted warehouses serve as modern lofts and a local coffee joint is never far away. But like the rest of the city, Lincoln Park has weathered various extremes over the years. After the Great Fire of 1871, new tract housing in the area served as a means to get citizens back on their feet. Years later, when the families moved out, the abandoned buildings would serve as an open invitation for squatters.

Chicago's manufacturing economy was booming in 1919 when the brick-and-mortar building at 1800 North Clybourn Avenue was built. After the Depression, the building would house local businesses, including a famous car wax manufacturing plant and, years later, a three-story shopping mall. Even so, housing projects and crime stories remained the neighborhood's dominant newspaper headlines for decades.

CLYBOURN
Grows up

John Hall never imagined the walls that housed his fledgling Chicago startup would ever be outgrown. It was a sign of how far not only Goose Island, but also beer appreciation overall, had come over the course of three decades.

In 2017, we closed the Clybourn location for renovations. The Clybourn Brewpub remains a revered part of Goose Island's local Chicago history and will be dearly missed as it undergoes a historic renovation and expansion. Once reopened, tours will be offered for visitors to enjoy the "original" Goose Island experience in its historic location.

When John Hall stumbled upon the property, small businesses were back on the rise, but 1800 North Clybourn hardly had the approachability of the typical 1980s sports bar. It would take someone willing "to jump into the deep end of the pool," as John says, to see the potential at a time when light beer and baseball were the only requirements for a neighborhood watering hole.

THE CLYBOURN AREA AT THAT TIME

was basically empty lots and abandoned cars, the shadow of a housing project. It was such a gutsy thing to do, all just because John wanted to do it."

—John Wyzkiewicz, former Goose Island brewer
Founder and brewmaster, Miskatonic Brewing, Greater Chicago Area

A Little Island Called
GOOSE ISLAND

Yes, there really is an island called Goose Island.

William Ogden, an influential businessman and Chicago's first mayor, also happened to open the city's first brewery. In 1853, Ogden's privately owned Chicago Land Company purchased a portion of the Chicago River and commissioned the excavation of a new North Branch channel to aid in clay extraction for brickmaking. The new channel created a man-made island that became home to a handful of industrial factories and Irish settlers during the manufacturing era. Initially nicknamed Ogden Island, the land was eventually dubbed Goose Island by locals, likely due to the flocks of geese kept by the early Irish communities. (This early Irish settlement was dubbed "Kilgubbin," named for the area in County Cork, Ireland, from which many of these settlers had emigrated. It was also the name of an Irish Red Ale available at Clybourn in the early days of the brewery and, for a limited time, bottled at the Fulton Street Brewery.)

Activity on the island was fairly limited, with a handful of manufacturing businesses dominating the landscape. More recent revitalization efforts have led to expanded residential complexes and a crop of new businesses on the island, including Kendall College, Chicago's longstanding culinary arts, hotel management, and business school. In 2005, the college moved its campus to a refurbished former Sara Lee warehouse on the island. (If you've been to any Goose U education events, you may have been there.)

The island's newfound role as a center for culinary education set the path for an unexpected food and beer pairing. Chicago's revered Siebel Institute of Technology (see page 44), the internationally acclaimed brewing and fermented beverage school, relocated to Kendall College's Goose Island campus in 2013.

 **The OGDEN**

We named our first Belgian-style tripel The Ogden in honor of the city's first mayor and brewery owner and the creator of the actual Goose Island in the Chicago River. The dry-hopped ale has spicy, tropical flavors and a bold, complex palate thanks to a uniquely Belgian yeast strain.

- THE -

OGDEN

BELGIAN STYLE TRIPEL

HONKERS Ale

*Honkers Ale has endured the test of time—it remains one of Goose Island's most iconic styles, and it's still popular today. **Lincoln Park Lager, Honest Stout,** and a handful of other classics occasionally reappear on tap at our brewpubs. All of our historical recipes have been slightly modified to take advantage of the best quality ingredients available today.*

Earning a Master of
BEER APPRECIATION

A boundary-pushing brewpub where you can hang with a great local beer, grab a bite, meet folks, or hole up and plug in? These are the denizens of "best of" lists today. In the early days of the brewery, things were different.

The inaugural tap offerings in 1988 were bold for the time (Honkers Ale, Golden Goose Pilsner, Lincoln Park Lager, Old Clybourn Porter, and Honest Stout). To those accustomed to watered-down pilsners, it was the equivalent of serving a decadent flourless chocolate cake to a customer with boxed cake mix expectations.

"You have to keep in mind that this was back when people hadn't tasted much of anything other than light lagers," recalls John. And so he came up with the Master of Beer Appreciation tasting program as a way to introduce new beer styles to a broader audience. The more beers tasted, the more "credits" earned towards an MBA.

Education, it turns out, really works.

"GOOSE ISLAND,

especially the Clybourn location, was the epicenter of all kinds of things going on in beer. Even before I became a professional brewer, as a home brewer, every time I came to Chicago, I'd show up at Clybourn and taste through all the beers. I'd take notes, and take that back home. It was a true learning experience."

—Matt Brynildson, former Goose Island brewer
Brewmaster, Firestone Walker Brewing
Paso Robles, California

MASTER OF BEER APPRECIATION CARD

The official Master of Beer Appreciation degree has been awarded to the most adventurous tasters at our Clybourn location nearly since we opened. With every fifteen "credits" or tastings, Goose Island MBA apprentices earn a free 64-ounce growler fill-up. (Research, all for research.) After forty-five tasting credits have been collected, the participants are granted a (very unofficial) Goose Island MBA. Working on an MBA comes with other benefits, like first dibs on tickets to Black Friday (page 128), the annual release of Bourbon County Brand Stout, and tastings of limited-edition beers available only on tap. Sure, the MBA program requires living in or near our Chicago campus, or visiting often. An excuse to drink unique beers and hang out in an incredible city? We don't see that as a problem.

" THE FOLKS AT THE CBS [CHICAGO BEER SOCIETY]

have been some of the best supporters of Clybourn and also played an instrumental role in creating and fostering the culture of Clybourn and beer culture in Chicago. Up until Clybourn closed for renovations in 2017, this group still held "Thirst Fursday," their monthly gathering, there. A week still rarely goes by that I do not get stopped by a member of the CBS telling me a fascinating story of their connection to Clybourn.

—Jon Naghski
Head brewer
Goose Island Clybourn

" WE ARE VERY LUCKY

to have the support of the Chicago Beer Society, which has been around since the 1970s. I think they were excited that we were making not just one or two, but five different styles of good-quality beer. Having that local encouragement early on from people who appreciated good beer kept us moving forward."

—Greg Hall
Goose Island brewmaster 1991–2011
Founder, Virtue Cider Company
Greater Chicago Area

Greg
HALL

Goose Island Brewmaster 1991–2011
Founder, Virtue Cider Company, Greater Chicago Area

Greg Hall got his start at the original Clybourn Brewpub. His glorious position at the company his father founded? Barkeep. Not the fancy kind who sports three-piece suits and shakes up trendy cocktails today, but the guy who washes dirty glassware and cleans up the place.

Like many of our brewers, Greg was driven by curiosity to learn the craft of brewing from the ground up. He honed his skills on the job, and pushed the limits of his skills in ways that have become synonymous with the name Goose Island. In the twenty years he served as Goose Island Brewmaster, Greg passed on that knowledge and passion to the dozens of brewers he mentored who now serve in top brewing positions worldwide. Greg's commitment to brewing a quality, innovative product remains fundamental to our core mission at Goose Island. His contributions to our company and the brewing industry as a whole endure.

"I really grew up at Goose Island, really formed who I am at Goose Island. It will always be part of me," says Greg. "What I've learned about brewing, and people, and Chicago, and beer will never be forgotten. Goose Island for me will always be 'we' and 'us,' and I'm proud of that."

Greg's contributions to Goose Island over the years are too numerous to count, but if he has a hall of famer, it's Bourbon County Brand Stout. The story behind the beer is as much about Goose Island's longstanding, no-holds-barred approach to uncharted territory as it is about simply wanting to brew a really great beer, and changing the way the beer industry approaches barrel aging.

"

I'M PROBABLY ONE OF
THE VERY FEW

of Goose Island's production brewers who can make the claim that Greg Hall taught me how to brew. And that experience has been about as valuable as it comes. The Halls provided this kind of once-in-a-lifetime opportunity to work in a modern brewery with an insatiable demand for products and a real desire to make classic examples and to also break through and make new beers for a blossoming craft beer scene."

—Matt Brynildson
Former Goose Island brewer
Brewmaster, Firestone Walker Brewing
Paso Robles, California

A BARREL OF AN IDEA
FOR A FINE AGED STOUT

The impetus to try our hand at making a completely different type of beer, the beer that would become Bourbon County Brand Stout, didn't come to life around an office conference room table. As with so many of our beers, the idea to age beer in bourbon barrels evolved in what some might call a more organic way—in this case, around a dinner table.

In the early 1990s, Goose Island was still earning its marks as one of the best breweries in the Midwest. Brewmaster Greg Hall, a self-proclaimed "numbers guy," wanted to make something special for the brewery's thousandth batch of beer. There was only one problem: he had no idea what to brew.

"Goose Island was asked to participate in a beer, bourbon, and cigar dinner in South Bend, Indiana, so I went," recalls Greg. "I got to sit right next to Booker Noe... now, that doesn't happen every day. Booker had been the Master Distiller at Jim Beam for a long, long time. We talked all night long about beer and bourbon. By the end of the night, I had managed to get six bourbon barrels from him."

Necessity may be the mother of invention, but barrels layered with the (truly breathtaking) funk of oak, smoke, and spices fueled something else entirely. "I got back to the brewery and said, 'Okay, we are going to make the biggest Imperial Stout we can, put it in bourbon barrels, sit back, and see what happens.'"

Our barrel-aging program continues to honor its roots with our original Bourbon County Brand Stout. Today, the series includes three additional core brands: **Coffee, Proprietor's,** and **Barleywine,** with special releases available in select years. Each is aged for up to one year in our Barrel Warehouse (see page 50). To this day, every release celebrates the innovative nature of that very first batch that found an aging home in any nook or cranny Greg Hall could find. For details on these and more beers in our Bourbon County series, see Our Beers, pages 116–133.

Creating a recipe for a beer that could stand up to the earthy, woody, bourbon-soaked character of those former Jim Beam barrels was an impromptu undertaking. There was no other brewer to call for advice, no other brewery's beer to taste that might offer clues of what profile might play best.

"I went all in, and stuffed more malt into the tank than I had ever done before," continues Greg. "This thing fermented so fast, in a couple of days," continues Greg. "At that point, I wasn't sure if that was a good thing or not." Greg left the barrels to age anywhere he could find space, which meant leaving them and their contents exposed to the elements.

Chicago's dynamic weather conditions—otherwise known as bone cold winters and beer-worthy summers—turned out to be the perfect barrel-aging environment. Weather fluctuations cause the wood to expand and contract, pushing the beer into the pores of the wood and back out again. "When the stout finally came out of the bourbon barrels, we knew this was a whole different type of beer. Nobody had ever made a [commercial] beer like it."

That much was true. The inaugural Bourbon County Brand Stout was bottled and submitted in the category of Imperial Stout at the Great American Beer Festival. "We got disqualified."

"This beer that we'd just been messing around with for our thousandth batch was too big, too strong, and too bourbon-y and barrel-y for what the beer judges expected. And then other people at the GABF couldn't stop talking about it. The character, the complexity, the flavors and aromas—people weren't used to experiencing these kinds of things in a beer."

The beer that sparked such flavor contention would go on to fuel an entirely new category of beers: barrel-aged stouts. To this day, barrel-aged stouts are one of the most prestigious categories at GABF, with competition among craft breweries for a medal in this highly skilled category a badge of (brewing) honor. The competitive drive around barrel-aged beer also spurned a Chicago-based, world class beer competition dedicated to the category: the Festival of Wood and Barrel Aged Beer (FoBAB). "And here we thought we were just making something for our thousandth batch that we'd never make again," says Greg.

For more on the barrel-aging process, see pages 78–79.

DOWN ON FULTON STREET

Mash tuns, fermenters, and wood barrels have a knack for taking up a lot of space. By the early 1990s, the original Clybourn Avenue brewpub location was beyond capacity. Our brewers needed a larger brewery and bottling plant to meet demand and have the space to work on our next creative brewing project.

In 1996, the new Fulton Street Brewery opened in the heart of Chicago's Near West Side, in the city's wholesale meat, fruit, and vegetable district west of the Chicago River. Today, the neighborhood has become a hub of innovative businesses. Our Fulton Street neighbors include Intelligentsia Coffee, a neighbor we tip our hat to each year in Bourbon County Brand Coffee Stout (see page 127), and more recently, a handful of up-and-coming breweries.

The Fulton Street Brewery has more than doubled in size since it was built. Today, our brewing headquarters contains everything we need to make our flagship beers and our latest innovations. To that end, the brewery includes the Wild Yeast Fermentation Room (see page 31) and the Pilot Brewery (see page 46) where our brewers have the creative license to brew whatever inspires them.

OUR Taproom

at 1800 West Fulton Street is typically open Thursday and Friday from 2 to 8 p.m. and Saturday and Sunday from noon to 6 p.m. Before you head down for a pint, be sure to check the website to confirm the hours, as special events or changes in hours may occur. Keep an eye out for special tappings and other community events in the taproom, from special tastings to homebrew discussions and chili cookoffs.

FULTON STREET TAPROOM

In 2015, we opened an intimate taproom at the production facility that holds around 120 people and has 80 seats. It's a place for locals to gather alongside Goose fans visiting from around the world. Special small-batch innovation releases that are only available at this location are on draft every week.

LOCAL COLLABORATION

Using local designers and sign makers, as well as repurposed materials, helped make the Fulton Street Brewery and Taproom a reflection of our Chicago heritage. Right Way Signs, which has been in business in Chicago for over forty years, painted the predominant mural on the outside of the taproom. Artisan Chris Knight of his namesake Chris Knight Creations handmade all the incredible wood signage you will find inside. Icon Modern, a manufacturer of custom sustainable furniture, crafted the one-of-a-kind tables and a giant bar top from naturally felled wood and reclaimed materials that measures more than thirty feet long. Other Chicago partners included Flux Studio and Hatch Design & Fabricate.

BREWING Facts

We bring you our pints using thirty-two fermenters, more than fifteen different yeasts, state-of-the-art filters, centrifuges, and (for the beer geeks out there) a fifty-barrel, JV Northwest five-vessel system that brews twenty-four hours a day, seven days a week. Our packaging line bottles five hundred cases an hour; our keg line fills fifty kegs every sixty minutes. Once bottled or in kegs, we store our beer at a crisp thirty-eight degrees until shipping to keep freshness at its peak. We use only the very best equipment and ingredients and—most importantly—the very best people to make our beer.

"THE FULTON STREET TAPROOM HAS BEEN

such an impactful addition to the brewery. For our fans to be able to share our story from the source, see our brewers in action, and sample new beers every week is the sort of community outreach we love to get our fans involved in at our Chicago home base."

—Jennifer Ohrn, Goose Island Beer Company experience manager

FULTON STREET BREWERY TOURS

Everyone at Goose Island was pretty excited about the taproom opening at our Fulton Street Brewery, and not just because a great beer can now be had by all after our brewers finish up their shifts or our office crew wraps up for the day. Okay, maybe that's part of the reason. (Hey, we all appreciate a really great beer around here.) The state-of-the-art facility means we can continue to push boundaries and brew the very best beer we can.

Tours are available on select days. Remember to book ahead at our website, as tours sell out in advance almost every week. www.gooseisland.com/tours

Learn
See the Pilot Brewery, where new brewing ideas come to life, and learn about the types of brewing yeast in our Wild Yeast Fermentation Room. Get to the heart of our barrel-aging process in the Barrel Warehouse.

Watch
Check out the live brewing action on the deck that overlooks our Brewing Operations and take a tour of our bottling line.

Taste
Taste samples of the tour tap offerings. Afterwards, settle in for a pint in the Taproom and then take home a complimentary Goose Island pint glass to explore uncharted beer territory on your own.

THE W FLAG: BEER & BASEBALL

Because we operate a brewery in Chicago, we were bound to combine two of the city's—and our—favorite pastimes. In 1999, Goose Island opened a brewpub and restaurant at 3535 North Clark Street in the Wrigleyville neighborhood surrounding Wrigley Field.

The two-story warehouse building was more than a temporary game-day hangout for Cubs fans. It became a neighborhood gathering place. For seventeen years, we served our flagship beers alongside experimental draft brews and the latest barrel-aging projects (including Cthulhu, a limited-release imperial oatmeal stout aged in an eighteen-year-old Elijah Craig bourbon barrel) with the same pride we have for our hometown and home team at Goose Island Wrigleyville.

When the building owner announced plans for a building renovation, we packed our bags and Pub Chips after the Cubs' 2014 season with mixed feelings of gratitude and sadness. Maybe it really was time to move on. When the renovations were delayed, we were right back there again for an unexpected replay in 2015. We like to think hanging in there "one more year" helped fuel our favorite team and city in some small way for what would come the following year: the Chicago Cubs winning the 2016 World Series Championship.

YOU CAN'T open a brewpub near a baseball stadium— especially in Chicago—without good snacks. At Goose Island Wrigleyville, the free baskets of salty-sweet barbecue potato chips, fried up in-house, had a cult following among Cubs and White Sox fans alike. For a home run pairing, try Four Star Pils or 312 Urban Wheat Ale.

GOOSE WRIGLEYVILLE BBQ CHIPS

Mix 3 to 4 tablespoons of your favorite barbecue spice mix, depending on the desired heat factor, with ⅓ cup of light brown sugar. Slice 4 to 5 medium, peeled russet potatoes about ⅛ inch thick. Use a mandolin for uniformly thin slices. Rinse the potatoes well in a colander until the water runs very clear. Drain them even more religiously on a kitchen towel (rustle them around a bit to make sure they are very dry). Fill a deep fryer with vegetable oil and preheat to 350°F. Fry the potatoes in small batches (do not overcrowd the fryer) until the potatoes are beginning to turn golden brown, around 5 minutes, depending on the thickness of the potatoes and the oil temperature. (Be careful once the chips begin to brown, as they can darken/burn quickly; light golden brown is the ticket.) Remove the chips with the fryer basket, transfer to a sheet pan, and immediately toss the chips with ⅓ cup of the sugar-spice mix to coat evenly. Add more spice mix to taste.

> ## "SINCE WE MERGED
>
> *with Anheuser-Busch, it's been great for us as brewers. We continue to operate with the same mantra of innovation and creativity, only we now have access to more ingredients than we ever did before: hops and malt, but also other ingredients like fruit for our sour ales, or whatever we feel like experimenting around with in a new Bourbon County Brand Stout blend. I can truly say we've never brewed better beers."*
>
> —Brett Porter
> Brewmaster, 2012–2015
> Head of brewing operations
> Goose Island Beer Company

THE ELEPHANT IN THE ROOM

Beginning in 2009, the Goose Island Beer Company began to face some substantial capacity issues and challenges. Market demand for our beers was greater than the ability of our brewery to produce and supply them. John Hall and his management team had to make some challenging decisions on how best to address the situation. The options boiled down to the following course of action: restrict Goose Island distribution.

For someone who loved sharing a good beer with others as much as John, Goose Island's founder wanted to avoid that fate, if at all possible. Nor did he want to eliminate any Goose Island jobs. Pulling out of markets would negate the years of effort and investment that it took to establish the brand in those markets.

Capital would be needed to install more brewing equipment at Fulton Street Brewery (see page 28), to explore the possibility of building a new brewery, or to expand the current Fulton location. Securing capital himself through private equity money was not a viable solution at the time (remember, this was just after the real estate market crash).

An "Angel" Investor

Around this time, and notably without solicitation, Anheuser-Busch InBev (ABI) contacted John. Their solution would allow Goose Island to maintain its distribution footprint, retain all of its employees, *and* have access to needed capital and brewing capacity.

Four short years after the acquisition, with the support of our parent company, our growth has significantly aided in the further development of the Fulton Street Brewery. We've added brewing equipment and a taproom, and exponentially expanded our Barrel Warehouse space and program. We have access to assets such as analytics and raw materials for brewing that undoubtedly would not have arisen without a parent company with the resources of ABI. We have more new jobs, not fewer. The relationship with ABI has allowed Goose Island to get more of our great beers to more people with plenty of exciting plans for the future. Today, our portfolio of beers is available in all fifty states and is expanding worldwide.

Elk Mountain
FARMS

Tucked away in a secluded valley in northern Idaho is Elk Mountain Farms, where many of Goose Island's best hops are grown and harvested. The farm is located on the forty-ninth parallel, which it shares with historical hops growers in Munich, Germany, and neighboring European regions.

In 1987, fourth-generation farmer Ed Atkins planted his first hop varieties on this land, and he has led the crew of hops growers ever since. Ed shares the same passion and commitment to quality as our brewers. Together, we have worked to grow the farm from a seventy-acre operation on the verge of collapse to a 1,700-acre hops sanctuary—the largest contiguous hops farm in the United States.

At 1,700 acres, Elk Mountain Farms is the largest contiguous hops farm in the United States (the average US hops farm is less than 450 acres; the largest grower in the Hallertau region of Germany is less than 200 acres). Harvest typically runs from August through October, depending on the variety of hops.

Hops cultivation on American farms hasn't been easy. These are finicky plants. The heirloom varieties our brewers get excited about require patience, experience, and perfect conditions to thrive: hot summers and, just as importantly, cold, wet winters. Over the years, Elk Mountain farmers turned to wheat and other crops when American craft beer palates were not as developed or attuned to hop flavors as they are now. Farms like Elk Mountain struggled to compete with bulk growers that churned out the sturdiest varieties.

Goose Island brewers have priority access to the hop varieties grown at the farm before they are offered to any other breweries. This allows our brewers to brew the very best beers and experiment with new styles.

Growing varieties of hops as meticulously as Atkins and his crew do racks up at a cost of almost $70,000 per acre, but that's a small price to pay for the opportunity to experiment with uncharted hop varieties at Goose Island today and in the future.

Today, the Amarillo used in Goose Island's Sofie is the largest hop varietal grown at Elk Mountain Farms, which currently grows ten commercial hop varietals. Atkins acknowledges Goose Island for driving the innovation that's happening: Elk Mountain Farms is currently growing 108-plus experimental hop varieties. With support from Goose Island, the farm recently built a micro processing plant onsite so those experimental hops can be used in small quantities and are also available immediately (it typically takes at least three years for a new hop planting to provide a good enough yield to process). You can feel—and smell and taste—the excitement when those experimental hops arrive at Goose Island's Pilot Brewery (see page 46). It's all worth it when the flavor stars collide and they end up in an upcoming release for our seasonal Experimental Beer Series.

Elk Mountain Farms Hops in Goose Island Beers

Goose IPA Cascade, Centennial

312 Urban Wheat Ale Cascade, Mt. Hood

Four Star Pils Mt. Hood

Sofie Amarillo

Green Line Pale Ale Mt. Hood, Millennium

Bourbon County Brand Stout Millennium

See which hops are used in which Goose Island beers in the details on each in the Our Beers section. For more on the history of hops and how they are used in beer, see pages 39–40.

THE 10 COMMERCIAL HOPS
Grown at Elk Mountain Farms

Amarillo
Cascade
Centennial
Hallertau
Millennium

Mt. Hood
Nugget
Saaz
Sorachi Ace
Willamette

The World of Hops

Beyond the variety, the location where hops are grown affects the hops' characteristics (similar to wine grapes).

Continental or Noble Hops

Noble hops originated in central Europe and are among the most prized of the aroma hops. Much as certain styles of beer may be called such if they were made in a certain region (Dortmunder must be brewed in Dortmund, and a true Trappist ale must be brewed on the premises of a Trappist monastery by the monks themselves), noble hops may officially be considered "noble" only if they were grown in the areas for which the hop varieties (or races) were named.

Flavor profile: spicy, black pepper, licorice, perfume, floral, herbal

English Hops

Most traditional English hops varieties fall into the low alpha acid aroma hops category. The most famous is the fuggle hops variety, long used in British ales. Many modern hops strains were developed from English varieties.

Flavor profile: herbal, grassy, earthy, floral, fruity

New World Hops

Bright, fruity, and resinous: these are the signature hops of American pale ale and IPA. New World hops are true to their name, as they were developed more recently in the beer history timeline and typically have bold profiles.

Flavor profile: citrus, grapefruit, resinous, piney, fruity, spicy

HOPS: AN ABBREVIATED WORLD TOUR

Ancient History: The use of hops in beer is a relatively recent innovation in the many thousands of years of brewing history. Originally, beer was flavored with various wild herb and spice mixtures (gruit) that added bitterness and various other flavors. These flavorings, like rosemary, ginger, spruce, and juniper, are still added to some beers today.

Eighth & Ninth Centuries: The earliest evidence of hops production in Germany dates to AD 736. Statues documenting routine monastery operations from AD 822 featured one of a Benedictine abbot who appeared to have gathered sufficient hops for making beer. Within a hundred years, hops were widely cultivated by monasteries.

Thirteenth Century: Exportation of hopped German beer began.

1629: Hops production was brought to North America by home-brewing Dutch colonists. Early American brewers used wild hops, though Old World hops production would soon influence New World beers.

1710: The English parliament banned the use of non-hops bittering agents to prevent evasion of a penny-per-pound hops tax. Hops became the dominant bittering agent throughout the Western world.

Mid-1800s: The US center of hops production moved from New England and Virginia to New York State. A mildew epidemic in 1909 nearly wiped out the state's production. Shortly after the state recovered around 1920, another mildew outbreak followed by Prohibition shut down New York hops production entirely. Farmers in Michigan and Wisconsin began growing hops but faced the same wet weather mildew outbreaks. The Pacific Northwest and California would soon become the home of US hops production.

Twentieth Century: Washington, Idaho, Oregon, and California became major worldwide hops producers.

Today: California and western Washington hops production has virtually ceased. Oregon and Idaho account for about 25% of US production, while the producers of the Yakima Valley of Washington make up most of the remaining 75%. Together, the Pacific Northwest states of Oregon, Washington, and Idaho's panhandle—where Elk Mountain Farms is located—grow more than 97% of the hops in the US.

HOPS Trivia

Hops become dormant over the winter, concentrating all of their energy in their roots.

Hops sprout in the spring and grow very rapidly—up to twenty inches per week—during peak summer growing season.

Hops always grow clockwise.

On hops farms, the bines (not vines) grow up heavy twine or rope, but in the wild, they use other plants for support to help them reach sunlight.

"Hop twine" (used to tie the bines to trellises) is called Coir Fiber, which is extracted from the husks of coconuts; it is biodegradable and can be tilled back into the soil after the harvest.

It typically takes three years for a hop plant to reach full maturity.

Young spring hop shoots are considered the most expensive vegetable in the world, can be cooked like asparagus, and were a specialty in ancient Rome.

GOOSE LESSONS

Embrace the Unknown

First and foremost, we are beer lovers. At Goose Island, we are honored to share our curiosity, expertise, and passion for great beer. Our future is perhaps best described with a word we use often: *innovation*.

We take pride in being an incubator for discovery, but innovation doesn't have to mean something entirely new. Innovation begins with a solid foundation, both on-the-job and, when available, through a more formal brewing education. This concept is also rooted in our dedication to changing how we approach the environmental resources that we all rely on every day (see Green Goose, page 45).

More literally, innovation can mean throwing virtually anything our employees dream up into the brew pot (see Fulton & Wood, page 49). It also involves embracing an existing idea, like barrel aging, and continuing to take those beers into uncharted territory.

BREWING AN EDUCATION

We believe education is the foundation of creative success. This is not only so we can make the very best beer, but so the next generation of brewers and our community can do so as well. Education is something we must work toward every day. From the brewery's earliest days, we have encouraged our brewers to acquire a deep understanding of the brewing process.

Much of that education comes on the job and is passed down from one brewer to another. It also comes from professional institutes. We have been lucky to share the great city of Chicago with the Siebel Institute of Technology, the world's premier brewing and beverage technology school.

GOOSE ISLAND

was basically the Midwest brewing school for me and a lot of other brewers still in the industry today. Every day was a learning experience."

—John J. Hall, former Goose Island brewer
Brewmaster, Metazoa Brewing, Indianapolis

OVER THE LAST
25 YEARS, *we've had so many great brewers here*

at Goose Island. The first couple of brewers left us for other jobs, and I really felt something was awry when I wasn't able to convince them that their best opportunity was to stay here. Later, I understood that not unlike myself, many of them wanted, and were now ready, to go off and start something different in the industry. We gave them a platform to go off and do all of those things. I now take great pride in the fact that our former brewers are working in many of the best breweries today, and many have started their own breweries."

—John Hall, founder
Goose Island Beer Company

THE SIEBEL INSTITUTE OF TECHNOLOGY

Established in 1872, the Siebel Institute and its affiliate the World Brewing Academy are respected as the premier institutes for international beverage education. It's no coincidence that each of the cities where degrees or courses are offered—Chicago, San Diego, Montreal, and Munich—are known as innovators in the beer industry. Alumni of these institutions can be found at the top breweries throughout the world.

In 2013, the Siebel Institute moved its local campus to the first floor of Kendall College on Chicago's (actual) Goose Island (see page 18). The convenient location near our Fulton Street Brewery solidified the bond between two brewing industry leaders.

COMMITTED TO INNOVATION

The ideas have been flowing—and, when things go awry, sometimes overflowing in the mash tun—ever since our very first days.

Innovation Team

We launched the Innovation Team nearly ten years ago. The goal of this "team of brewers" was to directly foster an environment where creativity was not only encouraged, but also considered a part of our daily mindset. This team has now been expanded into "Research and Development" of new and old styles alike, creating and recreating.

Pilot Brewery

We created a dedicated space for all employees to participate in the experimental idea-making process: the Pilot Brewery.

This is where the research and development for our brews happens, from the latest Bourbon County Proprietor's Blend variants to potential new Fulton & Wood beers (see page 49). It's where we try out new ingredient ideas (like fruits and spices), experimental hops, and other innovations. Countless recipes have been tested in that tiny brewhouse.

To see the Pilot Brewery firsthand, take a tour of the Fulton Street Brewery headquarters (see page 31). The latest experimental concoctions are often available to taste in the Taproom.

Collaboration Series

The creative projects aren't limited to our current employee roster. We have reunited with several of our former brewers to make collaborative beers, including Matt Brynildson of Firestone Walker, who developed Goose IPA while he was a brewer with us, and Phil Wymore at Perennial, who helped develop Madame Rose.

Each year, we also turn to local musicians to brew a beer for Chicago's Pitchfork Music Festival (see page 143). We have even worked with a renowned beer historian to revive a historical ale style because we wanted to find out what a stock ale might have tasted like (see page 143). Innovation is as much about history as it is about the future.

Goose Island Research and Development Manager

Yes, there is such a job at Goose Island, and yes, we all secretly want it. The Innovation Manager is an experienced brewer who acts as the creative bridge for the entire brewing team, from the cellar assistants to the brewmaster. He or she helps bring everyone's new—and sure, sometimes crazy-sounding—ideas to life in our Pilot Brewery.

ONE OF MY PROUDEST MOMENTS *being at Goose Island was helping come up with Juliet, which was the first innovation beer from the newly formed Innovation Team. The Innovation Team allowed us to play around with some things we'd never done at Goose Island before; we brought in some wine barrels, started aging in wine barrels in addition to bourbon barrels. We didn't know what the end result was going to be."*

—Matt Lincoln, former Goose Island brewer
Director of brewing operations
Fremont Brewing, Seattle, Washington

BREWING UP INNOVATION

When Goose Island founder John Hall moved the brewery to its current, much larger location at the corner of Fulton and Wood Streets in Chicago, he brought the same passion for brewing the very best, experimental beers possible along to the brewery's new, expanded headquarters. (For more on the early days of the brewery, see page 11.) Since then, we have expanded our Fulton brewery headquarters further, but one thing has remained the same: our commitment to innovation.

With these beers, we put the seed of innovation into the hands of our employees. And not only our brewers; every single person who works for Goose Island can participate. No matter how much our company has grown over the years, we stay true to our Bourbon County Brand Stout roots in believing that the very best ideas do not happen in a boardroom.

The Fulton & Wood Method

The creative process begins in countless ways: after a twelve-hour marathon horror flick spree, while watching some (crazy) Chicago surfers brave the waves of Lake Michigan in the dead of winter, or while recalling the impact of a 500-year-old beer law over a cup of really good coffee—or beer.

Each story and each beer is unique. A Berliner Weisse like Lilith, with her pomegranate "fruit of the dead" vampiress roots, Shred the Gnar, an Imperial IPA driven to big, hoppy West Coast surf-culture extremes with a Midwestern tart cherry twist, or 1516, a Bavarian-style Rauch-Kellerbier brewed in honor of the 500th anniversary of Germany's Beer Purity Law.

From there, a team of employees forms organically, and the group lays out the aroma and flavor profile with a handful of our brewers. Finally, the winning ideas are turned into experimental brews in the Pilot Brewery (see page 46). The results are first available for tasting on draft in the Chicago area and at a handful of special events.

The very best go on to a nationwide release, like the cucumber-infused C.A.L.M. Radler and clove-scented Rasselbock (a culture mashup of a doppelbock, roggenbier, and Bavarian weiss), along with new seasonal releases each year.

For more on the Fulton & Wood series and releases, see Our Beers, page 145.

> # "HAVING THOSE EXPERIMENTS,
> *the times when the brewer can be free and play with what they want, to create whatever flavors and styles they are inspired by, is such a luxury. Everyone gets to participate, not just a few top brewers. Every once in a while, you'll have this amazing new beer that comes out of it. It could be brewing with tea, or brewing with alternative yeast strains, or different brewing processes all together. That way of continuing to push the boundaries, of learning what **can** be done with beer and not necessarily what **has** been done with beer, is so important."*
>
> —Tom Korder, former Goose Island brewer
> Co-founder and brewmaster
> Penrose Brewing, Greater Chicago Area

A BARREL-AGED VISION

In the early 1990s, a small Chicago brewery made craft beer history with the first bourbon-barrel-aged beer (for more on the story behind the first Bourbon County Brand Stout, see page 26). Today, Goose Island is world famous for its barrel-aging program. We have more than 130,000 square feet of barrel-aging warehouse space filled with bourbon, whiskey, and wine barrels, and, more recently, foudres.

"CREATING
OUR BARREL-AGED BEERS,

from the brewing process to blending the beers after aging, is as much art as it is science. It requires an incredible amount of patience and skill and is truly a labor of love."

—Mike Siegel
Former Goose Island brewer and cellarman
Brewing innovation manager
Goose Island Beer Company

GOOSE ISLAND BARREL WAREHOUSE

In 2014, we opened the Goose Island Barrel Warehouse a few miles from our brewery on Chicago's West Side. The entire space was designed and built to the specifications of our brewers, with more than 130,000 square feet dedicated to the art of barrel aging beer.

After being brewed and fermented at the Fulton Street Brewery, the beer is transported two miles down the road to the Barrel Warehouse on a dedicated tanker truck. The beer is then pumped into one of two stainless steel tanks. Our brewers fill the barrels, and the beer settles into its residence in this incredible barrel-aging facility.

Bourbon Barrels

Our brewers choose barrels that have held sweet whiskey in their bellies for a minimum of four years, and then they age our beer inside for eight to twelve months. This process takes place in a non-climate-controlled space, allowing exposure to the extreme heat and cold of Chicago's ecosystem, which contracts and expands the wood, pulling the wood's whiskey character into our brew. Each barrel is used only once, ensuring the best quality taste in every pint.

The first Bourbon County Brand Stout was brewed in the early 1990s, but it would be some years until Goose Island had the capacity to brew and bottle the beer commercially (the first release was in 2005). Today, our Bourbon County Brand Stout portfolio includes a half dozen core and special-release beers. In 2017, we celebrated the beer's historical beginnings with a Bourbon County Reserve Brand Stout aged in eleven-year-old Knob Creek barrels—the straight bourbon that Jim Beam founder Booker Noe created.

With our Cooper Project, a rotating series launched in 2017, our expertise in bourbon barrel aging will be taken to exciting new places with our annual twists on traditional beer styles.

For more on the Bourbon County portfolio and Cooper Project, see Our Beers, pages 126–149..

Wine Barrels

Three years after the first retail Bourbon County Brand Stout release, we expanded our barrel-aging program again. This time, our brewers brought wine barrels into the experimental picture. They started with beer that had undergone primary fermentation in stainless steel casks before transferring it to wine barrels. Additions of fresh fruit and wild yeasts initiated a secondary fermentation inside the barrel, followed by nine to eighteen months of patient aging, depending on the beer.

The process yielded beers with an unprecedented depth of character, increased acidity, and a light essence of tempered fruit aromas and flavors not unlike a fine wine. The various unaged oak wine barrels we use now yield some of our most unique brews, including Sofie and the Sour Sisters: Juliet, Lolita, Madame Rose, Gillian, and Halia. For more on Sofie and the Sour Sisters, see pages 96 & 102–115.

The Brasserie Series of beers, launched in 2017, takes our wine barrel–aging program in a new direction with Chateau Noir, an imperial stout aged in cabernet barrels for a red wine–like profile, and Chateau Blanc, a golden ale aged in first-use wine barrels with Riesling grape juice for dry white wine attributes.

With our Fulton & Wood series and collaborative one-off projects, we never know where an unexpected collaboration might go. An extremely limited release of Sofie aged in two very different barrels from Philadelphia winery Karamoor Estate Wines (one previously used to age a Cabernet Franc, the other a Petit Verdot)? Why not? For more on our Fulton & Wood and Collaboration series, see page 135.

Other Barrels & Foudres

With our passion for bourbon and wine barrels, it was only a matter of time before our brewers were enticed by other barrel-aging opportunities. We've used rye whiskey barrels to make special releases like the 2015 Bourbon County Regal Rye. We've even used our own flavor-rich barrels in special releases like Bourbon County Rare Barleywine, a 2017 release made with Bourbon County Barleywine aged in our 2015 Bourbon County Brand Rare barrels. These American white oak barrels were originally used to age bourbon for more than thirty years.

With the Foudre Project, a series of limited-release beers aged at our barrel-aging warehouse in oak foudres (large wooden vats traditionally used to age French wine like Bordeaux), we take the "barrel" aging concept in a completely different—and much larger—direction for a more subtle infusion of woody characteristics. For more on special Bourbon County releases and our Foudre Project, see page 140.

THE BEER

*We brew the oldest beverage in the world...
yet our story is just beginning.*

BREWING 101

Beer is a carbonated drink made from fermented grains, hops, yeast, and water— simple, right?

Wine is made from one ingredient: grape juice. Beer has much more complex beginnings, starting with cereal **grains** that have been malted. Barley is the traditional grain used in brewing, but oats, rye, wheat, and other grains are also common. **Hops** are added for bitterness, aromatics, and subtle flavor notes, and **yeast** is used to induce fermentation and in the process provide vastly varying aromas and flavors. Depending on the style, **adjunct ingredients** like fruits, herbs, spices, or extracts can be added to bring other characteristics to the brew. And let's not forget the most important ingredient: **water**.

WHAT'S ON TAP

For the most part (because beer has an exception for every rule, as it should), beer is either an ale or a lager. Even some of our boldest experiments over the years (see page 46) usually fall into one of those two categories.

Ale

An ale is defined as a beer that uses yeasts that have been propagated and cultured to both hold up to higher temperatures (60 to 75°F) and ferment at the top of the fermentation vessel.

The ale fermentation period occurs more quickly, around seven to ten days, causing ales to often—but not always—have higher residual sugars and aromatics due to the quicker fermentation process.

Lager

A lager is beer that relies on yeasts that have been propagated and cultured to brew at lower temperatures (34 to 50°F) and ferment at the bottom of the fermentation vessel. Lagers typically take more time to ferment than ales. The process can take a few weeks or months; the word *lager* comes from the German word *lagern,* which means "to store." (Today's advanced tank technology, specifically cylindro-conical tanks, have helped reduce lager fermentation time; filtration techniques can speed up the maturation time.) Lagers often have a crisp taste because they have fewer residual components after fermentation.

THE HISTORY OF BEER In One Paragraph!

Good luck with that. Suffice it to say that the 9,000-plus years of global brewing and toasting history have centered around religious rituals and beer goddesses (and no doubt a few sacrifices we don't want to know about), tainted water supplies (fermentation is a form of sanitation), and plenty of memorable culinary moments—all before we get to the first beers brewed on American soil.

MALTS

Cereal grains that have been roasted after going through the "malting" process

The word *malty* is often used to describe certain beer styles (for more about the flavor, see page 59). In terms of the brewing process, malt is primarily responsible for three things in a finished beer: **color**, **alcohol content**, and **richness/mouthfeel**.

The Malting Process

"Malting" prepares the starch in the grain for conversion into fermentable sugar, which acts as food for the yeast during the brewing process. To "malt" a grain for brewing, cereal grains (typically barley) are soaked in water until they begin to germinate and sprout, which synthesizes starch degrading enzymes within the grain. After soaking, the grains are kilned to halt the germination process by reducing moisture, and are prepared for storage. After this process, the grains are known as "green malt."

Kilning/Roasting The green malt is then kilned or roasted at varying temperatures and lengths of time to reach the desired color and flavor profile. In the old days, the sun was used to roast the grains, but today, hot air kilns—or sometimes smokers—are used instead. Roasting levels vary from a very pale straw color (base malts, 2-Row, Pilsner, Pale, Munich) to the darkest black (chocolate malts, debittered black malts, roasted barley) and everything in between.

Brewing When mixed with hot water during the process of mashing, enzymes synthesized during germination convert the grain starches into water soluble sugars. These sugars, along with the colors and flavors of the selected malts and cereal adjuncts, result in a liquid that is separated from the mash solids to become "wort," the base for the production of beer. During fermentation, the yeast consumes the wort sugars, creating alcohol, carbonation, and heat as byproducts.

Color

The color of a beer is primarily determined by the degree to which the malts are roasted before they are used to brew beer. For details on the role color plays in the appearance of a beer, see page 149.

Malt Aromatics & Flavor

"Malty" is probably one of the most common words used to describe beer, but it is somewhat of a misleading term. Malt lends beer a color in addition to contributing to the alcohol content and residual sugars.

The aromas and flavors beyond sweetness are typically more indirect but are present in almost all beer styles. In the least, malt provides a variety of subtle but key grainy tastes like sourdough and biscuit. That grainy, cereal-like, or "husky" flavor can be a dominant quality, especially in some stronger ale styles like nut brown ales, porters, and stouts. The malt grains can also contribute to the perceived dryness of a beer because like hops, husks of malts do contain some tannins.

COLOR WHEEL

Beer newcomers tend to shy away from darker beers like stouts and porters because they look more "intense," but in blind taste tests, the sweeter, malty notes—oatmeal, chocolate, toffee, and similar—in those beers were exactly what novice beer drinkers preferred. Beers with a pronounced bitterness, like most IPAs, look "lighter" but tend to be a stronger, acquired taste that develops over time, like that for black coffee.

UNLIKE HOPS, which act more like herbs and directly contribute aroma and flavor qualities to different styles, malt's aroma and flavor are derived primarily from a secondary source: the brewing process.

Malty aromas are a result of the caramelization* of the sugars that malt produces. How much of the husk is used, how finely milled the malt is, the temperature at which and length of time the wort is boiled, and other factors all contribute to the presence of "malty" aromas and flavors in a finished beer.

*Though the word caramelization is often used in describing brewing malts, true caramelization requires much higher heat than is typically used in brewing. The process is technically a Maillard Reaction, a chemical interaction between amino acids and reduced sugars in the wort due to heat exposure.

Common Terms

Malt Aromatics Dough (especially sourdough), biscuit, freshly baked cookies

Malt Flavor Bread, cereal, grain, caramel, molasses, toast, roasted barley, smoke, charcoal

Richness / Mouthfeel

What is often described as a malty "flavor" in a beer is actually the sweetness that your tongue picks up from the **residual** sugars that remain after the brewing process is completed (for more on mouthfeel, see page 159).

Typically, residual sugar is determined by the amount of sugar not consumed by the yeast used to ferment the beer—more malt can mean more sugar byproducts. Those sugars give some beers a malty-sweet richness and creamy mouthfeel, as in many stouts and porters.

The use of more malt contributes to the potential for increased alcohol content, which affects the weight of the beer. The type and amount of hops, the yeast strain and attenuation, and the addition of such sweeter added ingredients as fruit also influence mouthfeel.

↑ Malt + ↑ Sugar Byproducts = ↑ Alcohol + ↑ Sweeter Taste

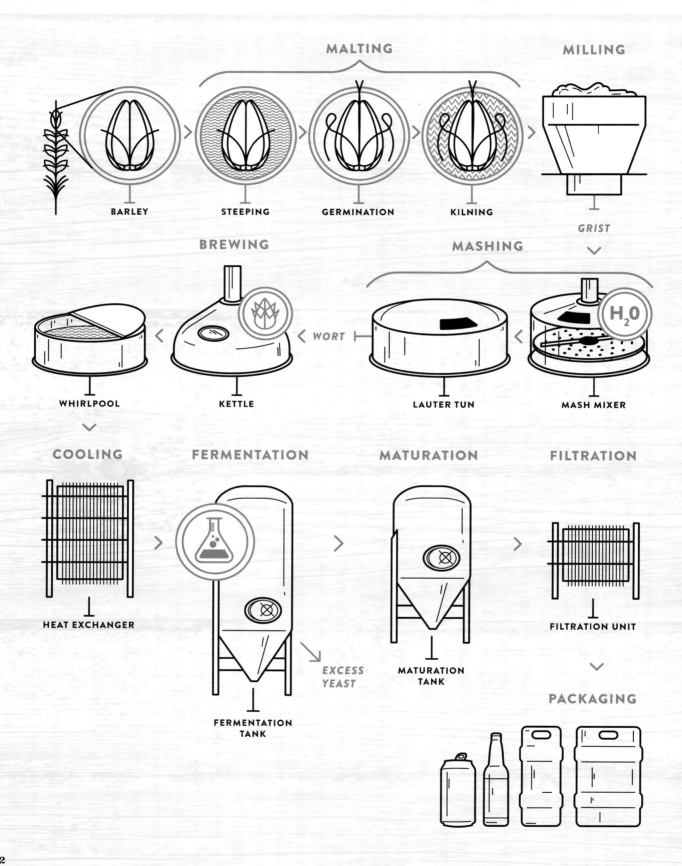

MALTING

MILLING

BARLEY STEEPING GERMINATION KILNING

GRIST

BREWING

MASHING

H₂0

WHIRLPOOL KETTLE WORT LAUTER TUN MASH MIXER

COOLING FERMENTATION MATURATION FILTRATION

HEAT EXCHANGER

EXCESS YEAST

FERMENTATION TANK

MATURATION TANK

FILTRATION UNIT

PACKAGING

THE BREWING PROCESS

These are the basic steps to brewing beer. Some styles, like sour ales, include additional steps (other ingredient additions, wild yeast fermentation).

Malting the grains
First, the grains that will be used as fermentables in the beer are germinated, dried, and roasted

Milling
The husks of the grain are cracked to varying degrees; a traditional grist mill is typically used (mills like hammer mills are used when a different grain consistency is desired)

Mashing the grains
The milled grains are steeped in hot water so their sugars can be extracted

Lautering and sparging
The malt husks are strained from the liquor, and then hot water is run through the grain bed to extract a sweet liquid called wort

The Boil
The wort is brought to a boil in the brew kettle

Hops are added at different times during the boil to give the beer bitterness, aromatics, and flavor

Fermentation
After the boil, the hopped wort is cooled through a heat exchanger and transferred to a fermenter, where yeast is added or "pitched"

Over time, the yeast will consume the sugar in the wort, producing alcohol and carbon dioxide

Maturation (brite tank)
The fermented beer is transferred to a secondary tank, also known as a brite tank, in which the beer is matured, clarified, and mildly carbonated

Filtration
The beer is run through a filtration unit that clears the beer, removing yeast, proteins, and particulates that could produce undesirable flavors in the beer

Barrel aging
Some beers are then put through an additional conditioning/maturing process in wooden casks (typically second-use barrels that have previously housed other spirits and wine)

Depending on the beer style, fruit, wild yeast, and friendly bacteria may be added during this stage

Packaging
After additional carbonation is added, the finished beer is typically packaged in half barrels (15.5 gallons), barrels (5.2 gallons), 750ml bottles, 12-ounce bottles, and 12- and 16-ounce cans.*

*Packaging size varies today; Goose Island uses 765ml bottles and 16.9-ounce bottles for select releases.

"CRAFTING A PRODUCT THAT BRINGS SO MANY PEOPLE TOGETHER

has been my dream ever since I can remember. I love being able to directly interact with beer lovers. One of the most exciting, humbling, and crazy experiences I get to partake in as a professional brewer is working at a craft beer event. I used to be on the other side of the booth as a consumer, asking for beer, hoping for a taste of something new and exciting. Now, I get to serve that excitement to people. I have so much fun pouring, joking, and being a part of someone's best day ever. I once lost my voice after pouring at a beer event. I couldn't stop talking about the beers!"

—Emily Kosmal, Goose Island brewer
(Hoplightsocial.com, September 13, 2016)

HOPS
The flavorful seed cones (flowers) of the
Humulus lupulus plant

Hops act as a natural **preservative**, which was handy in the days before refrigeration. Today the plant is mainly celebrated for its incredible **flavors** and **aromas**.

Flavor
All of those residual sugars from the malts and other ingredients are countered by the pleasant **bitter** flavor of hops. Alpha and beta acids contained in the soft resins of each hop cone react to the heat of the boil during the brewing process to create what our palate perceives as a bitter taste. The natural tannins in hops can also influence what is described as a **dry** finish in some beers.

Beyond bitterness, hops are an incredible source of other subtle **flavors**, from citrusy to grassy and so much more. The variety and quantity of hops, the steeping process (see page 66), and aging all play a role in the degree to which bitterness and other flavors are detectable in the final beer.

For more on flavors and tasting, see page 153.

International Bitterness Units
International Bitterness Units (IBUs) is a scale measuring the perceived bitterness of a beer. The number scale relates to how much dissolved **isomerized** alpha acid from the hops is present in a finished beer. The higher the number, the higher the concentration of bitter compounds in the beer. A lighter beer like a pilsner might have an IBU of five on the scale, while some double IPAs might clock in at eighty or more. Like tea, the variety of hops used, what type (fresh or dry), and how long the hops were left to steep in the wort play a role in the perceived bitterness of a beer. Even when a beer has a high IBU, it may not taste particularly bitter due to other qualities in the beer like residual sweetness from malts and aging.

IN CHEMISTRY
In chemistry, **isomerization** is the process by which one molecule is transformed into another molecule which has exactly the same atoms, but which have a different arrangement. In brewing, alpha acid in hops will only contribute to bitterness if it has been chemically altered or isomerized to its water soluble structure. During brewing, the alpha acids in hops are isomerized in beer through the boiling process.

A NEW (AGED) BEER
Looking at the ingredient list and statistics like the IBU of a barrel-aged beer can be deceiving. For example, each batch of Bourbon County Brand Stout utilizes twelve pounds of hops and five thousand pounds of malt (a blend of six different types). The finished beer has a relatively high IBU—around sixty, the same as Goose IPA—but the bitterness is balanced by the beer's more dominant characteristics like nuttiness, caramel-like notes, and other bold flavors. Aging also plays a key role as the perceived bitterness will reduce over time. The end result is a beer that does not have the dominant, hop-forward aromas or flavor of an IPA.

Aroma

Hops are packed with delicate **aromas**. The flowers of the plant contain lupulin glands, which are responsible for the flavors but also a sea of incredible aromas. Rub a fresh hop bud between your fingers, and you can feel the resins and essential oils inside those glands sticking to your fingers. (This is more fun than it sounds!) You will also smell all of the great, subtle characteristics of whatever hop variety you are holding.

Preservative Quality

Like salt and lemon juice, hops are a natural preservative. Unhopped ales only lasted a few weeks before beginning to sour (a desirable quality for only a handful of current beer styles). Considering the nearly 10,000-year history of brewing, hops are a relatively new discovery (herbs, flowers, and other ingredients were used for flavoring beer). The first documented use of hops was not until the ninth century, though it would be another seven hundred years before brewers in countries like England would use hops as a preservative and flavoring agent. One of the most popular craft styles today, the IPA, was developed with the preservative quality of hops as a key feature (for more on the history of the IPA, see page 84).

NUMBERS GAME

The big, rich stouts in the Bourbon County Brand Stout series are a good example of the complexity of the brewing process—and interpreting the meaning of a beer's **International Bittering Units** (page 65). Most of the Bourbon County beers clock in with high IBUs (60), yet they don't taste overtly bitter. The elevated bitterness is masked by all of the complex malty and aged flavors in the beer. After cellaring, the beer's "detectable" IBU drops substantially, and the rich, nuanced flavors of the beer dominate. In much lighter beers with lower IBUs, like Goose IPA (55), the bitterness is front and center on the tongue.

LEADER OF THE PACK

The scientific name of the hop plant, *Humulus lupulus*, means "wolf amongst the weeds"—a she-wolf. The plant's female flowering cones, called strobiles, are the "hops" part of the plant used to make beer.

The Steeping Process

Hops are as sacred to brewers as grapes are to winemakers. The variety of hops and how a brewer handles them, along with other ingredients and aging, have key influences on the final flavor of any beer.

Variety of Hops Like all produce, each variety of hops is unique. Some have much higher levels of bitter-producing alpha acids, while others are particularly piney, earthy, or even grapefruit-like. We are in the middle of a hops revival in the United States, with an incredible variety of hops at our fingertips (for more on the specific varieties grown for Goose Island beers, see Elk Mountain Farms, page 35).

Steeping Process Ever brewed tea? Both the length of time the hops are boiled and the temperature affect final flavor. To make a light, balanced pilsner, the hops are steeped briefly and at a lower water temperature, which is typical of lagers (see page 58). This results in a balanced beer that is not too bitter, with more subtle flavor characteristics from the hop variety. A very hop-forward beer like an IPA is steeped at much higher temperatures—as are all ales—and for a longer time before straining.

Adjunct Ingredients / Aging Process As with malty sweetness, perceived bitterness is affected by adjunct ingredients that may mask some of the flavor qualities in the hops with sugars (as from fruits) or other dominant flavors (spices, coffee, tea, and similar). The length of time a beer is aged and the aging vessel also play a role. A metal tank is not going to mask bitterness, whereas a beer aged in a woodsy bourbon barrel will have more of its bitter flavors mitigated.

Hops
& THE BREWING PROCESS

Hops are typically added to wort in one to three stages during the boil: bittering, flavoring, and aroma. As usual, there are exceptions, especially these days, with so much brewing creativity. Some beers may have only one, while others may have five or more additions. All beers do have at least one hop addition ("bittering") to balance the sweetness of the malt.

STAGE 1: BITTERING "Bittering" hops are added once the wort has been collected in the kettle and a rolling boil has been achieved. They are typically boiled for as little as forty-five minutes or for up to two hours to extract the most bitterness, although the time varies depending on the beer.

STAGE 2: FLAVORING "Flavoring" hops are generally added when there are between fifteen and thirty minutes remaining in the boil. In this time frame, less of the bitterness will be extracted and more of the crisp, subtle hoppy flavors will be imparted to the boiling liquid. The time that they are boiled again makes a flavor difference. The hops used may be the same variety used as the "bittering" or "aroma" hops, or the brewer may choose a different variety.

STAGE 3: AROMA The hop oils that are responsible for aroma are extremely volatile. They dissipate in the hot steam of the boil very quickly, so aroma hops are boiled very briefly. They are typically added during the last few minutes of the boil, or after the heat is turned off, which works like taking a boiling pot off the stove.

OTHER HOP ADDITION METHODS Hops can be used in brewing in other ways, too:

DRY HOPPING This is the most common non-boil use of hops. "Dry hopping" refers to adding hops to beer at some point in the process well after fermentation has begun. Dry hopping imparts an incredibly fresh hop aroma and character to the beer without adding much, if any, bitterness.

FIRST WORT HOPPING The pre-boil addition of hops to the hot wort as it runs into the kettle from the mash/lauter tun is known as "first wort hopping." Some brewers think that this process gives a smoother hop aroma and flavor without significantly increasing bitterness.

HOP, SKIP...

A "hop back" is a small tank that is placed between the kettle and the chiller in a brewing system. It is filled with hops so that the hot wort can run through the tank on the way to the chiller. The process imparts more subtle flavors and aromas and is typically used along with other hops addition methods.

YEAST

Single-cell organisms that convert sugar into alcohol and carbon dioxide

None of those malty, hoppy, and other fantastic nuances we love in beer would be possible without yeast. As a colony of living cells, yeast's primary purpose in the food and drink world is to eat fermentable sugars. (Tough job.)

Saccharomyces cerevisiae is the strain typically used in both brewing and baking, though different strains are used to make some beers. To brew sour or "wild" ales, *Brettanomyces* yeast strains are the most common, which is why they are sometimes referred to as "Brett" sours or "Brett" beers. The wild yeast gives those beers incredibly complex, nuanced flavors, but also makes them finicky to brew. Regardless of the type of yeast used, those yeast sugar cravings leave several desirable byproducts in the finished beer.

Determining Beer Style

Specific yeast strains create certain flavors and aromatics that are quintessential to a certain style of beer. For instance, Bavarian wheat yeast contributes esters that impart the banana, clove, and bubblegum characteristics that Bavarian Hefeweizen is known for, and Saison yeast is what gives Sofie some of its floral and peppery qualities.

> # " I WAS THE CELLAR MAN
>
> *who had to deal with the* Brettanomyces *when we were developing Matilda, which was all really 'green' [new] to us at the time. We were worried we'd end up with a lot of bad batches because of the wild yeast, so we came up with a 'plan' that pretty much consisted of me cleaning a tank for eight hours straight. And Matilda was still by far my favorite beer to make during my time at Goose Island."*
>
> —Will Johnston
> Former Goose Island brewer and cellarman
> Brewmaster, 4 Hands Brewing Company, St. Louis

BRETT PORTER,

Goose Island Beer Company's former brewmaster (who now oversees Goose brewing and several other craft brands), has both a sour ale-worthy first name and a last name that calls for a British pint. (The porter style became popular in London in the nineteenth century.) Cheers!

Carbon Dioxide In baking, the **carbon dioxide** that helps bread rise is "baked off" during cooking. In brewing, it is the opposite: when the malt sugars are consumed by yeast, the carbon dioxide remains in the beer and creates bubbles known as **carbonation**.

Foam The "head" on a beer is caused by the carbon dioxide bubbles rising to the top of the drink and being released into the air. The amount of foam varies depending on the type of beer and how it is poured into the glass (see Glassware, pages 170–173). A pilsner or light ale will typically have more foam than an aged stout, but as always, it depends on the beer. Again, the opposite is true for many aged stouts and similar beers. Note, the attributes from cereal grain choices will heavily influence the foam production and head retention/foam stability of the beer in a glass.

Both **cask-conditioned** ales and **nitro beers** (beers with added nitrogen) typically have an almost creamy, smoother texture than most beers because they release much smaller carbon dioxide bubbles. The nitrogen taps traditionally used for Guinness create that same "creamy" mouthfeel.

BARMY!

The brewer-baker camaraderie goes back thousands of years. In England, bakers would go to brewhouses to buy the yeasty, carbonated foam left over from brewing (called *barm*) and use it to make savory sandwich buns called barm cakes.

Alcohol In bread baking, heat "kills" the alcohol the same way it does with carbonation. Like carbon dioxide, the alcohol created by the yeast remains in a finished beer. (Carbon dioxide can also be added to the finished beer.)

ABV The alcohol content by volume, or ABV, of a beer is influenced both by the amount of malt used (remember, more malt means more sugars) in the brewing process and what types of adjunct ingredients (fruits or sugars like honey) might be tossed into the mix.

Other factors, like how long and how a beer is aged—in a vessel like a barrel, or even longer in the bottle—also affect the final alcohol content of the beer.

Esters Yeast doesn't typically get much credit beyond fermentation, but the chemical compounds that yeast emits during the brewing process, called **esters**, are also responsible for many of the aromas and flavors we love.

Some ester combinations are more **fruity** (figs, plums, strawberries), while others are **herbaceous** (sage, thyme), **flowery** (jasmine, honeysuckle), or **spicy** (black pepper, cinnamon, cloves).

Phenols Also known as carbolic acid, phenols are a class of chemical compounds responsible for several common flavors and aromas. One phenol is responsible for the distinct smell of cloves, nutmeg, cinnamon, and vanilla; one for the smoky notes in coffee; another for the distinct smell of freshly crushed berries; and so forth.

These qualities can be desirable or not, again depending on the style of the beer. The wonderfully spicy, clove-like character in a Belgian Dubbel is in part thanks to phenols. "Off" flavors in beer that was poorly made or has spoiled can also be the result of phenols: the smell of Band-Aids, the taste of plastic, and others. Chlorine is often the culprit; the chlorine in water or in brewery cleaning products can react with the yeast in beer to create the phenols that cause these aromas and flavors (see "Off" Aromas, pages 74–75).

WATER
Self-explanatory (we hope)

At Goose Island, we are very lucky to have the abundant fresh water of Lake Michigan at our fingertips. As the site of a massive glacial reservoir, the Great Lakes supply what we believe to be world class brewing liquor for the beers we brew in Chicago.

Hard versus Soft Water
There are two basic types of water. What is known as **hard water** has a high concentration of minerals like calcium, magnesium, zinc, copper, and sulfates, while **soft water** is relatively low in minerals.

Historically, whether a beer was brewed in an area with hard or soft water sources likely influenced what style of beer was typically brewed, from a light Pilsen-style beer in the Czech Republic (where water is softer) versus the richer stouts in England (where the water tends to have more minerals). Water is only one of a number of factors that came into play as new beer styles developed, including the preferred foods of each region.

Today, brewers make so many different styles of beer, from the lightest Kölsch to the boldest stout, that the "type" of water is less influential. So many things have changed since the first beers were brewed. Beyond technological advances, brewers today have access to the same quality of ingredients year after year—including clean, sustainable water.

Unfiltered Beer
The yeasty aromas and flavors from all of the esters are particularly noticeable in unfiltered beers. Most beers have been filtered after brewing to remove most of the yeast compounds. Filtering tends to make beers taste lighter or "cleaner." Examples of unfiltered beers with fantastic yeast notes include unfiltered wheat ales and sour ales brewed with wild yeast, like the Sour Sisters.

"Off" AROMAS & FLAVORS

Brewing is a science as much as an art. What reviewers describe as "off" aromas and flavors can also be desirable in some beer styles. While there are many undesirable aromas and flavors, these are some of the most common.

OFF FLAVOR: ASTRINGENT

Although they don't look it, grains are delicate and require delicate handling. The oils in the germ of the whole grains used in brewing are more readily spoiled by heat, light, and moisture than those in finely milled grains like flour. The flavors packed in the husk and germ are also sensitive to how the grain is processed. Over-milling or over-crushing brewing grains without proper equipment to handle them, or over-steeping or sparging grains with boiling (too hot) water can cause a super mouth-puckery, cotton-mouthy astringency.

Exceptions: Astringency is sometimes desired in certain styles, such as IPAs, although the astringency in an IPA should be derived from hop tannins and not tannins from barley skins.

OFF FLAVOR: VEGETAL

Dimethyl Sulfide, known as DMS for short, can present in a really bad way. It can taste like cooked corn or boiled cabbage. Even worse, it can have notes of seafood and shellfish, which are fairly unacceptable in any beer style. While this off flavor naturally occurs in brewing, it is released from the beer through evaporation during a vigorous boil and fermentation. If condensation from the boiling portion of brewing rejoins the wort, or if fermentation isn't rigorous or allowed to finish, an unacceptable amount of DMS can remain in the beer.

OFF FLAVOR: BUTTERY

One thing yeast loves when it begins the fermentation process is oxygen. While it's only good to aerate your beer at certain times during the brewing process (just before and after pitching the yeast), a lack of aeration at this time can cause flavors that have buttery or slick butterscotch notes. This off flavor is known as diacetyl, which is also the natural byproduct used to make artificial butter. While yeast naturally creates diacetyl during fermentation, only healthy yeast will adequately reabsorb it to clean it back up at the end of fermentation. The addition of oxygen at the beginning of fermentation promotes healthy yeast growth. Not adding enough yeast to the wort can also be a culprit.

Exceptions: Small amounts of diacetyl are acceptable in some beer styles, particularly in traditional older English beer styles.

OFF FLAVOR: FUSEL

Except for a couple of specialty yeast strains, most beer should be fermented below 80°F. High temperatures can kill yeast and in addition produce harsh, hot gasoline–like flavors and/or solvent characteristics. Brewers call this off flavor fusel or fusel alcohol.

OFF FLAVOR: OXIDATION

While early yeast aeration is essential, after the fermentation process, oxygen can destroy a beer's aromas and flavors. Oxidation can occur at any time in the post-fermentation process, especially when a beer is transferred to storage or aging vessels or to bottles. Off flavors from oxidation can contribute wet dog and cardboard flavors and aromatics.

Exceptions: Oxidation is acceptable in some styles like some old ales, barleywines, and barrel-aged beers.

IS IT CLEAN ENOUGH OR TOO CLEAN?

Sanitization is essential at any food or drink production facility, and perhaps even more so at a brewery. Bacteria is the number one source of off flavors in beer. Cleaning equipment is especially important when wild yeast is involved, as natural yeasts can easily create off flavors not expected in a non-wild beer style. Just to make things even trickier, cleaning products can also cause off flavors due to chlorine or other antiseptic ingredients. This is why brewery equipment is always rinsed well with water after cleaning.

OFF FLAVOR: ACETALDEHYDE

A beer described as "young," meaning the yeast was strained off too soon from the brew, and the fermentation process doesn't have a chance to completely finish, can have flavors and aromas of green Jolly Ranchers, nail polish remover, or tart green apples (bacteria can also be to blame). This off flavor is called acetaldehyde.

OFF FLAVOR: SULFUR

A beer that sits on the yeast too long will eat all of the residual sugars available, including other yeast (very much like a sourdough starter will do). Yeast autolysis includes yeast cannibalism and the actual breaking down of the yeast cell itself in addition to the hydrogen sulfide that yeast naturally produces during fermentation. This process can result in a taste of rotten eggs, which has often been described as the worst of the off flavors in beer.

OFF FLAVOR: SKUNKY

A beer typically tastes "skunked" as a result of a chemical reaction that takes place when ultraviolet (UV) light interacts with hop components in the beer that are invisible to the naked eye. This is why darker brown bottles and even cans are universally preferred today; both marked turning points in beer preservation history.

OFF FLAVOR: PLASTIC

Whether a local water source is hard or soft, as well as its dominant flavor characteristics, has played a role in determining the style of beer in different regions throughout history. A water source can also be the cause of "off" flavors. Chlorine is often the culprit. It reacts with the yeast in beer to create phenols that evoke medicinal, smoky, or plastic-like flavors and aromas.

OFF FLAVOR: GROSS

Bacterial and/or wild yeast infections can produce any and all of the off flavors: astringent, vegetal, buttery, fusel, oxidation, acetaldehyde, sulfur, skunky, plastic, or, as we like to say, "just plain gross." These funky aromas and flavors may evoke corn and cabbage or old bandage and spoiled milk.

ADJUNCT INGREDIENTS
Other ingredients added during or after the brewing process

Beer is arguably more experimentation-friendly than any other beverage (yes, wine, we are talking about you). If it's edible, it's likely been in a brewing experiment somewhere, sometime—maybe even in our **Pilot Brewery** (see page 46).

Beyond the unique flavor notes, the **amount** of the adjunct ingredient that is used and the **intensity** of those flavors (mild or strong) will have the most significant effects on detectable flavors in the finished brew. Intensity is partly determined by the ingredient itself, and partly by the process used to extract the flavors.

As with hops, flavor intensity of adjunct ingredients is determined by the length of time an adjunct ingredient is left in a beer, when an adjunct ingredient is added (when the wort is hot or during the aging process, when the beer is room temperature), and how long the ingredient is left in the mixture (briefly or never extracted, as in many aged fruit sours). Adjunct ingredients that are high in sugars, like fruit, can also affect the **alcohol content** of the finished beer. Common beer-friendly adjunct ingredients include:

Fruit Berries (strawberries, blackberries, myrtle/juniper berries), stone fruits (cherries, peaches), pome fruits (apples, pears), citrus (peel or juice: oranges, lemons, grapefruit, yuzu, bitter laraha), melons (cantaloupe, honeydew, watermelon), tropical fruits (coconut, pineapple, mango, tamarind, and similar), dried fruits (currants, raisins, apricots, prunes)

Vegetables Light vegetables (cucumbers), sweet vegetables (beets, pumpkin, sweet potato), spicy peppers (serranos, habaneros, jalapeños)

Herbs / Spices Fresh herbs (chamomile, dill, rosemary, sage, spruce, pine), fresh spices (ginger, lemongrass), dried spices (cloves, coriander, cumin, nutmeg, star anise)

Sweeteners Agave syrup, brown sugar, honey, maple syrup, molasses

Extracts and Other Flavorings Vanilla and nut extracts (almond, hazelnut, pecans), liquid smoke, coffee, chocolate, peanut butter, tea (unique blends like kombucha, lapsang souchong)

The Barrel-Aging Process
Barrel aging and aging in general have been part of the brewing process for longer than even historians are likely to say. Today, we think of barrel aging in terms of the incredible complexity the process adds to the beer's aroma, flavor, and overall enjoyment, but the process also helps preserve and protect the beer, which was essential in the days before refrigeration.

Difficult as it is for us to believe, Goose Island has been barrel aging beer for more than a quarter of a century. It all began with the very first batch of Bourbon County Brand Stout (for more on that story, see page 26). Later, we began experimenting with the Sour Sisters and Belgian-style ales like Sofie. Most recently, we launched the Cooper Project. All are brewed and aged with the same commitment to quality.

For detailed information on each of our barrel-aged beers, see Our Beers, starting on page 116.

"ONE OF MY FAVORITE VARIANTS OF BOURBON COUNTY BRAND STOUT

was the Backyard Rye with mulberries that we hand-picked [released in 2013]. It was aged in Templeton Rye whiskey barrels with fresh mulberries, marionberries, and boysenberries. The next year, we tried nine different versions of Bourbon County Rye variants, most of which were rejected. One of the worst was my idea to use wild Oregon huckleberries. It sounded like a good idea from the berry success the year before. It was awful. The flavor of the seed dominated the flavor of the beer. We also tried a chili beer that ended up with an oil slick on the top of it and burned your mouth for at least two hours. You have to go through that tasting process to get to the best. It doesn't happen by just saying what you think will be great."

—Brett Porter, brewmaster, 2012–2015
Head of brewing operations, Goose Island Beer Company (Reddit interview)

BARREL-AGING
THE THREE MAJOR COMPONENTS

ANATOMY of a BOURBON BARREL

1. The Char Layer: Contributes smoke, chocolate, and roasted coffee flavors to the beer.

2. Absorption Layer: Flavors of tobacco, leather, and tree bark come from this layer.

3. Bourbon Layer: Coconut, caramel, vanilla, and cherry flavors are imparted by this layer.

4. Raw Wood Layer: Contributes earthy and woody flavors to the beer.

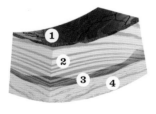

EXTRACTION: FLAVORS IMPARTED by the BARREL

Barrel expansion in warm temperatures.

Barrel contraction in cold temperatures.

CELLARING & the AGING PROCESS

The Angel's Share and Devil's Cut.

Barrel Preparation

All the bourbon barrels used for Bourbon County Brand Stout are filled and used "as is," meaning without rinsing or steaming before use. This preserves the aroma and flavor qualities of the previous liquid that was housed in the barrels (bourbon, wine, and similar) so they penetrate the stout.

For some of our other barrel-aged styles, our brewers do steam the barrels. With these beers, they are looking for the conditioning qualities of the porous wood rather than any qualities of the previous tenant (see Aroma & Flavor Development, page 79). We call these steamed barrels "neutral oak."

Weather Conditions

Warm weather causes wood to expand, allowing the beer to penetrate deep into the barrel's pores. In cold weather, wood contracts. This squeezes the beer back into the belly of the barrel, bringing the charred wood and bourbon character along with it.

Chicago's dynamic weather conditions—otherwise known as Imperial worthy cold winters and sessionably hot summers—turned out to be the perfect barrel-aging environment. To take advantage of the Chicago terroir, we age Bourbon County Brand Stout without internal temperature controls like air conditioning or heating. (Those knit caps our cellar men and women are sporting in videos aren't fashion statements.)

Evaporation & Absorption

Aging beer in a porous material like wood causes some of the liquid to evaporate during the aging process. This creates the rich, concentrated intensity of barrel-aged beers and contributes to the beer's complex aromas and flavors.

Angel's Share: The volume lost due to evaporation during the aging process.

Devil's Cut: The volume lost due to beer being absorbed deep into the barrel staves.

Aroma & Flavor Development

As with wine, barrel aging creates a unique vintage each year. The complex profile is comprised of the multiple, and very different, layers of flavor and aromas in the barrels. With neutral oak wine barrels, the flavors will primarily reflect the wood. Barrels that have been used for aging stronger spirits like bourbon will take on those characteristics as well.

Fruit and any other flavorings that are introduced to the beer as it ages also affect aroma and flavor development. Good examples include the Sour Sisters with fresh fruit, while beers like Bourbon County Brand Proprietor's Blend include fruit, spices, and other ingredient additions.

Bourbon Barrels

Bourbon County Brand Stout, Cooper Project, other experimental beers

Char Layer (smoke, chocolate, roasted coffee)
Absorption Layer (tobacco, leather)
Bourbon Layer* (coconut, caramel, vanilla, cherry)
Raw Wood Layer (earthy, woody)

*Other barrels previously used for spirits include rye whiskey barrels (Bourbon County Brand Backyard Rye, Cherry Rye, and others) and single-vintage bourbon barrels aged for more than thirty years (Rare Bourbon County).

Whiskey and other barrels are also now a part of our expanded barrel-aging program.

Oak Neutral Wine Barrels

Sour Sisters, Sofie, other experimental beers

Wood Layer** (earthy, woody)
Additions (fruit, spices)

** The Sour Sisters, Sofie, and most of our other wine barrel–aged beers are all aged in "oak-neutral" barrels, or those that do not retain the aroma and flavor properties of the wine. More recently, we have experimented with aging beer in barrels that do retain some of the qualities of the wine, as in the Brasserie Series (see page 53). With these, additional layers of flavor from the wine are imparted to the beer.

Blending & Bottling

After the designated aging time, which varies by beer, brewers start the process of tasting every single barrel in our Barrel Warehouse multiple times to determine whether that barrel is ready to "rack." Some brewers must taste hundreds of samples a day, a task that is much more difficult than it sounds. (Try swirling, tasting, and spitting a huge red wine over and over—it's a major palate killer.) Our brewers then rack, or empty, the barrels. Finally, the brewmaster blends the barrels together in batches. Each barrel lends a unique character to the liquid inside and the blending process is the magic that produces the final beer that reflects the optimal qualities of that year's vintage.

Bottle Aging

Barrel-aged beers can be enjoyed right away, though these beers develop complexity as they age in the bottle for five years or longer. At home or in a retail establishment, the ideal storage temperature is the same as the typical wine refrigerator, or around 55°F (for more on storing beer, see page 165). The exceptions are draft offerings of our barrel-aged beers, including Bourbon County Brand Stout, the Sour Sisters, Matilda, and others. Draft versions should be enjoyed within one year.

OUR BEERS

Our goal is to consistently brew beer of the highest quality that is distinctive in taste.

Goose Island Brewpub opened its doors in 1988. At the time, American light lager beer was deeply ingrained in Midwestern culture, and the craft beer industry was still in its infancy. Goose Island came onto the scene by brewing classic and traditional English-style beers: an English-style bitter and an India Pale Ale—quintessential recipes of quintessential styles. Both were a departure from the norm and startling to the American market.

Over the years, Goose Island has expanded that initial portfolio while staying true to our original mission to brew the very best beers. Today, we brew a range of beers. We offer an English-style summer ale as a nod to our roots, and we head to the continent to brew one of the most revered traditional styles of all: the pilsner, a lager that is worlds apart from those early American light lagers that served as the catalyst for a new kind of beer company. The beers in our portfolio today continue to be familiar yet surprising, recognizable yet also revelatory. We hope you will agree.

This brand guide offers details about the beers that exemplify our take on quintessential, traditional, and hybrid beer styles. Availability often changes as we experiment with new styles. Social media platforms are a good place to look for information on new releases, event information, and whatever else might be brewing at Goose Island.

Twitter   @Goose_Island

Facebook   facebook.com/Goose-Island

Youtube   youtube.com/user/GooseIslandBeer

Pinterest   pinterest.com/GooseIslandBeer

Instagram   instagram.com/gooseisland/

Tumblr   goose-island-agegate.tumblr.com

Vimeo   vimeo.com/user13103819

Snapchat   snapchat.com/add/goose-island

DEFINITION OF STYLE TERMS

ABV   Alcohol by Volume (alcohol content)

IBU   International Bittering Units: bitterness based on a scale of 1 to 100 (strain and quantity of the hops; see page 65)

COLOR   Appearance (amount the malt is roasted; see pages 159–161)

MALT   Strain(s) of malt

HOPS   Varietal(s) of hops

RATINGS

This tasting scale is based on the beverage industry standard.

95–100   Outstanding

90–94   Excellent; a beverage of superior quality

85–89   Very Good; a beverage with unique qualities

CLASSIC ALES

We got our start brewing ales, and they continue to be a style we strive to exemplify. The ales in this section are Goose Island classics. Whether they are more recent additions or have been in our portfolio for decades, each is distinctive in taste and brewed to be of the highest quality.

GOOSE IPA

A beer that can stand up to an 18,000-mile sea journey

In the eighteenth century, British brewers faced a shipping predicament. They needed to create a more stable product that could survive the long cargo ship journey from Europe to India, where a world of spices awaited—along with very thirsty soldiers and colonists. British sailors received a beer stipend for their significant travel commitment: four to six months, depending on the weather. To meet demand, a London brewer created a pale ale with more hops and a slightly higher alcohol content than was common at the time; like hops, alcohol acts as a preservative. These more aggressively hopped beers were called India Pale Ales, a reference to their destination.

Some historians believe the IPA's preservation and cargo-ship roots may have been exaggerated. They argue the increased hops level in those early IPAs was likely negligible, and stouts and other lightly hopped beers routinely survived the long journey across oceanic spice trade routes. The style may have developed more gradually, as a true flavor preference. Either way, these new, bold IPAs were here to stay.

Goose IPA was inspired by traditional English-style India Pale Ales. Former brewmaster Greg Hall wanted to create a beer that would push the creative limits of what American beer fans had experienced in a hop-forward beer. The year was 1999, five years before double IPAs (known as "West Coast IPAs") would be released commercially along the West Coast, and long before IPAs lined the taps of craft beer bars. The beer would go on to become one of the top three sellers in the Goose Island portfolio.

Style India Pale Ale
Goose Spin Fruity aroma set off by a dry malt middle and a long, balanced hop finish
Aroma / Flavor Citrusy, fruity aroma / dry hop finish
Overall Impression Bright and approachable bitterness

Reason to Believe With six gold medals to its name, to date Goose IPA has won more Gold Medals at the Great American Beer Festival than any other beer.

FROM SEED TO SIP

It takes time and care to brew a great IPA. A selection of the hops we use in Goose IPA is grown specifically for Goose Island at Elk Mountain Farms (see page 35). Fresh hops are handpicked at the farm and then sent to our brewers to make an award-winning IPA.

ABV	5.9%
IBU	55
Color	Bourbon
Malt	Pale
Hops	Cascade, Celia, Centennial, Pilgrim, Styrian Golding
Availability	Year-round; nationwide
Bottling	12-ounce bottle, 12-ounce can, 16-ounce can
Draft	1/6 and 1/2 bbl
Preferred Glass	Nonic pint
Cellaring Notes	Enjoy within 180 days

"I'M PROBABLY ONE OF THE VERY FEW OF GOOSE ISLAND'S

production brewers who can make the claim that [founder] Greg Hall taught me how to brew. And that experience has been about as valuable as it comes. I think Goose IPA is probably my personal crowning achievement relative to formulating a beer with Greg and seeing it all the way to fruition. Then, in 2000, it went on to win the gold medal at the Great American Beer Festival in its category."

—Matt Brynildson, former Goose Island brewer
Brewmaster, Firestone Walker Brewing
Paso Robles, California

"A STRAIGHT-UP, OLD-WORLD PILSNER,

with a light, golden hue formerly brewed in the Bavarian region of southern Germany and the Czech Republic, Four Star Pils uses a specific type of grassy hops grown in (or inspired by) those regions, giving the beer a slightly elevated bitterness. It also turns a traditional pilsner, which really works with lighter food like veal bratwurst, sushi, and roast chicken, into a beer that really cuts through richer foods like scallops, meat, and cheese. But one thing I really like to eat with this beer—I mean, a lot—is a good, old-fashioned burger. The hop character and malt background go really well with a burger. The drinkability is through the roof."*

—Jared Jankoski
Goose Island brewmaster, 2015 to present

FOUR STAR PILS
The most popular craft style today and one of the oldest European styles of beer

The pilsner style, sometimes spelled pilsener or abbreviated to pils, originated in Bohemia. At the time, the area was a province in the Austro-Hungarian Empire (now part of the Czech Republic). In 1842, German-speaking immigrants brewed the first known blonde lager and named it after Pilsen, a German city in the province.

The lighter lager style was later adapted by German brewers elsewhere, including in the United States. Pilsners fueled the early American brewing market and continue to do so today. Traditional German-style pilsners are brewed to be crisp and refreshing, with hops that tend to present more flowery, or less bitter, nuances. Done well, it is the quintessential sipping beer for a hot summer day.

With Goose Island's original portfolio of full-flavored, English-style beers, founder John Hall faced an unexpected wall of light lager expectation (see page 11). Today, sophisticated beer drinkers with an appreciation for a broad range of styles have fueled the revival of truly top-quality pilsners.

Our brewers experimented until we struck what we feel is the perfect twist on the classic American-style pilsner. Like many of our beers, some of the hops are sourced from our very own Elk Mountain Farms (see page 35). Four Star Pils has the crispness we craved in a pilsner with enough unexpected hops personality to fit our commitment to delivering the next great beer. With a unique profile and sessionable, refreshing qualities, it is perfect for any occasion, summer or otherwise.

Style American-style pilsner
Goose Spin Brewed with both American and German influences for a unique bitterness
Aroma / Flavor Crisp hop aroma / hop-forward, clean finish
Overall Impression Effervescent and refreshing

Reason to Believe **The pilsner category is the fastest-growing category in craft, with estimated 50% growth over the next three years.**

LIKE CHICAGO'S FLAG
the Four Star Pils label bears four embossed stars, one for each of the monumental events in the city's history: Fort Dearborn, the Great Chicago Fire of 1871, the World's Columbian Exposition of 1893, and the Century of Progress Exhibition in 1933/34. Our new Four Star Pils glassware includes a "y" at the base of the glass, representing the place where Chicago's river becomes two branches.

ABV	5.1%
IBU	38
Color	Light Golden
Malts	2-Row, Special Pale
Hops	Mt. Hood, Hallertau Tradition, Opal, Hersbrucker
Availability	Year-round; nationwide
Bottling	12-ounce bottle, 12-ounce can, 16-ounce can
Draft	1/6 and 1/2 bbl
Preferred Glass	Pilsner glass
Cellaring Notes	Enjoy within 180 days

312 URBAN WHEAT ALE
An urban take on a longtime favorite

An English-style summer ale is a variant of a classic style that struck out in the naming business: British ordinary bitter. Don't let the name fool you. The style is nothing like it sounds, but rather known for being balanced in terms of both flavor (not too bitter or malty) and alcohol. It is a true session beer (see page 92). These everyday draft ales were served at cellar temperatures through a hand pump or with the aid of gravity, meaning no external carbonation sources were used, as is common today. Modern tweaks to the style opened the door for pale malts, refreshing flavor tweaks, and more palatable names like golden ale or summer ale.

Our version of a summer ale, 312, was inspired by the city of Chicago and is densely populated with flavor and character. The unfiltered beer takes on the spiciness of Cascade hops with a fruit-forward flavor and creamy body but a refreshing finish, unlike any other ale style in the Goose Island portfolio. We felt it deserved its own (unofficial) style category: Urban Wheat Ale.

Style Summer ale
Goose Spin A blend of barley malt and torrified wheat creates a smooth, creamy body
Aroma / Flavor Crisp, lemony, and spicy aroma / fruity, smooth finish
Overall Impression Refreshing yet full-flavored

Reason to Believe In 2005, we launched a little beer called 312 that made craft beer accessible to the masses. It has won multiple gold medals at the Great American Beer Festival.

CHICAGO'S FIRST
area code, 312, remains the area code for the original Clybourn Brewpub and is the area code for the Fulton Street Brewery.

ABV	4.2%
IBU	18
Color	Hazy straw
Malts	2-Row, Torrified Wheat
Hops	Cascade, First Gold, Mt. Hood
Availability	Year-round; nationwide
Bottling	12-ounce bottle, 12-ounce can, 16-ounce can
Draft	1/6 and 1/2 bbl
Preferred Glass	Weizen (Weissbier) glass or nonic pint
Cellaring Notes	Enjoy within 180 days

"WE WERE PHASING OUT GOOSE ISLAND PILS,

and my idea to replace the pilsner was a light, unfiltered wheat ale. I wanted to make a hazy beer, but not hazy from yeast. I also wanted something kind of citrusy. That was the entire direction. From there, I did some investigation, talked to my master [brewing] friends, and came up with the recipe for 312. I never thought it would end up so popular."

—John J. Hall, former Goose Island brewer
Brewmaster, Metazoa Brewing, Indianapolis

"MAKE NO MISTAKE,

beers like Green Line were born in, and were inspired by, Chicago, but we don't try to hide the fact that we now brew some of our [more widely available beers] in New York and Colorado. Goose Island brewers—myself included—are still the ones leading the production of all Goose Island beers. The beers are made according to our brewing process and recipes, and we use the same ingredients. Each batch is vetted by our taste panel back in Chicago. When you scale up production, consistency of flavor is one of the most difficult things to maintain. I fully believe that we have never brewed, or been able to brew, better than we are right now."

—Brett Porter, brewmaster, 2012–2015
Head of brewing operations, Goose Island Beer Company

GREEN LINE
A Chicago area–only release with a wandering soul

American pale ales are a California invention. In 1980, the first West Coast commercial version was released as a variant on an English pale ale with a more pronounced hops presence. Today, the style runs the hop aroma and flavor spectrum, with breweries choosing hops with distinct qualities for their brews. The bitterness tends to be in line with an English-style IPA, which is typically less hop-forward than an American-style IPA.

Some American pale ales, like our version, clock in with a lower ABV than many hop-forward beers, making them immensely sessionable (see page 92). The biscuity qualities from the lightly toasted malt used in Green Line balance out the pleasantly bitter ale.

Style American-style pale ale
Goose Spin Highly sessionable with an original Chicago beat
Aroma / Flavor Hops and citrusy aromas / toasted grain backbone and crisp finish
Overall Impression Crisp with a pleasant bitterness

Reason to Believe A hometown rising star.

PART OF THE "L"
(elevated) metro train, the Green Line connects Chicago's South Side with Downtown and runs two blocks from the Fulton Street brewery. The Chicago draft version continues to be brewed at the original Fulton Street Brewery.

ABV	5.4%
IBU	30
Color	Wildflower honey
Malts	Special Pale
Hops	Millennium, Mt. Hood, Zythos
Availability	Year-round; nationwide
Bottling	12-ounce bottle, 12-ounce can, 16-ounce can
Draft	1/6 and 1/2 bbl (Chicago only)
Preferred Glass	Nonic pint
Cellaring Notes	Enjoy within 180 days

HONKERS ALE
The original

English-style bitters grew out of British pale ales. By the late 1800s, the style had become a popular draft offering at British pubs. The style highlights the bittering quality of hops, but despite the name, the style is not especially bitter in comparison with today's double IPAs. The name arose as a way to distinguish these beers from the sweeter, less hop-forward beers like stouts and porters that were popular at the time. (English brewers were hops holdouts. They were the last European brewers to introduce hops into their beers, having previously favored herb flavoring agents.) English-style bitters remain the most common "real ales" in England. This term refers to beers traditionally served very fresh and at cellar temperatures, without additional pressurized carbonation.

The Honkers Ale story is deeply rooted in English-style bitters pub history. After a trip to England, Goose Island founder John Hall had a craving for the beers he had tasted in countryside pubs. With none to be found, he decided to open a brewery from the ground up (see page 11). That was a beer-changing moment not only for our company, but also for Chicago beer drinkers and, years later, fans of well-crafted beers everywhere.

SESSION

The word "session" today can refer to any lower-alcohol beer. Originally, the British term referred to beers that could ride the wave of a continuous, multi-hour drinking session at a pub or similar without severe overindulgence effects. The word may also have its roots in British Parliament. Elected officials could drink the lower-alcohol style (beer was a common drink, like water) and supposedly keep a clear head.

Style English-style bitter
Goose Spin Truly a classic tribute to a time-honored and respected style
Aroma / Flavor Fruity hop aroma / rich malt middle and smooth finish
Overall Impression Balanced richness and bitterness

Reason to Believe Honkers Ale is a beer that truly respects tradition—and always has—at a time when craft brands are only beginning to appreciate balanced flavors again. One of Goose Island's very first recipes, the beer is still in production thirty years later.

NAMED BY

John Hall's wife, Patricia, Honkers Ale was inspired by their travels to England, where sessionable ales are common in countryside pubs.

ABV	4.3%
IBU	30
Color	Golden sunset
Malts	2-Row, Caramel, Roasted Barley, Wheat
Hops	Golding Celeia, Pilgrim, Styrian
Availability	Year-round; nationwide
Bottling	12-ounce bottle
Draft	1/6 and 1/2 bbl
Preferred Glass	Nonic pint
Cellaring Notes	Enjoy within 180 days

"I USUALLY TELL PEOPLE

that my favorite beer is the beer in my hand. And more often than not, there is a beer in my hand. But I'm probably a little partial to Honkers Ale because it was one of our original beers that survived. Also because it's a really great, flavorful beer without a lot of alcohol, which I think is important. Session beers, or lower-alcohol beers, are a fabulous style of beer."

—John Hall, founder, Goose Island Beer Company

BELGIAN-STYLE ALES

Belgian-style ales, from farmhouse-style ales to barrel-aged sours, were a natural progression for Goose Island brewers. Each of our Belgian-style ales is layered with subtle complexity. Savor a glass on its own or invite these remarkable dining companions to the table. They play well with others … especially good food.

SOFIE
Invite Sofie to brunch

Saison, or "season" in French, refers to a beer traditionally brewed around the town of Liège in the French-speaking part of Belgium. It was brewed by Belgian farmers in the winter for summer enjoyment to attract the best farm hands, who were given up to five liters a day as part of their compensation. Today, Saisons have enjoyed a revival, which many beer experts credit as saving the style from near extinction. Most are referred to as "farmhouse ales" because of their rustic, earthy, and subtly sour qualities, though the style can veer in various flavor directions.

Our version of a Saison is wine-barrel-aged with plenty of hand-zested orange peel (for more on the barrel-aging process, see page 81). The result is a bright, sparkling ale with spicy citrus complexity. Our goal was to brew an exceptional ale as inviting as the original Belgian Farmhouse ales, yet with the light, effervescent complexity of Champagne. It is a quality we hope the original French brewers would appreciate.

Style Belgian-style farmhouse ale, barrel-aged
Goose Spin Aged in wine barrel oak casks with hand-zested orange peel
Aroma / Flavor Spicy white pepper aromas / complex citrusy notes, creamy vanilla finish
Overall Impression Tart, dry, and effervescent

Reason to Believe A multiple medal winner at the Great American Beer Festival, Sofie continues to inspire. Brunch is the fastest-growing dining-out meal, with nearly half of diners ordering an alcoholic beverage. Beer is typically left off the brunch menu, but the Sofie-Mosa (see sidebar) offers an unexpected way to fill that void.

SOFIE was named after brewery founder John Hall's granddaughter. The beer is incredibly food-friendly and makes an excellent and easy brunch cocktail.

The Sofie-Mosa is a refreshing mix of freshly squeezed orange juice.

For that and more beer cocktail ideas, see pages 204-205.

ABV	6.5%
IBU	20
Color	Champagne
Malts	2-Row, Pilsen, Wheat
Hops	Amarillo
Aging	Barrel-aged 3 months; develops in the bottle for up to 5 years
Availability	Year-round; nationwide
Bottling	12-ounce bottle (4-pack)
Draft	1/6 bbl (limited)
Preferred Glass	Chalice or Goose Vintage Glassware
Cellaring Notes	Up to 5 years

LEGEND OF THE ORVAL FOUNDATION

The Cistercian monastery Abbaye Notre-Dame d'Orval was founded in 1132 in Belgium. The abbey name and arms design are credited to the widowed Mathilda of Tuscany. According to legend, Mathilda was traveling in Belgium when she lost her wedding ring in a pool of water near the future site of the monastery. When she prayed for the ring's return, a trout rose to the surface with the ring in its mouth. Out of gratitude, she donated a substantial sum of money to build a monastery on the site and proclaimed the location truly a "Val d'Or" (sacred Golden Valley), the root of the name "Orval." The abbey arms depict a trout with a ring. The original abbey was destroyed and rebuilt several times until its most recent renewal in 1931 as a Trappist brewery. Today, the abbey continues to produce its coveted Trappist-style Belgian pale ale, Orval.

MATILDA
A Trappist legend travels to Chicago

The Trappist style includes dubbels (doubles), tripels (triples), quadruples—words that roughly correspond to the amount of malt used in the brewing process and the alcohol level. The overriding quality of a true Trappist ale is that it must be brewed on the premises of a Trappist monastery by the monks themselves, not hired hands, and in accordance with traditional recipes. Brewing profits must be used solely for running the monastery or donated to outside charities. Many monasteries make at least one version for sale. One of our favorite Trappists is, like the monastery where it is made, called Orval, meaning "valley of gold." The monks there also brew a less alcoholic, or petite, version for themselves.

Today, Trappist-style ales have become wildly popular at non-monastic breweries, including Goose Island. American versions of Belgian-style ales obviously are not required to abide by historical standards, opening up the opportunity for experimental brewing. Our version, fermented with both Orval clone yeast and the wild yeast strain *Brettanomyces,* is fermented and matured in stainless steel rather than oak barrels. The resulting beer is bottle-conditioned to bring out its spicy flavors and phenolic aromas.

Petite Matilda

In 2016, Goose Island teamed up with James Beard Award–winning chef Paul Kahan for a special beer brewed for the 26th annual James Beard Foundation Awards. Just as

Matilda takes its inspiration from Orval, Chef Kahan, along with the Goose Island Innovation Team, created a recipe inspired by Petite Orval—the unassuming lower-alcohol beer brewed for the monks themselves and served only inside the Orval brewery in Belgium.

Petite Matilda, a Belgian-style session ale, took a modern diversion. It was dry hopped with the new German Hüll Melon hop, which balanced the lighter-bodied beer with fruity and peppery notes. Petite Matilda rang in at about 4.5% ABV and 20 IBUs.

Style Belgian-style pale ale
Aroma / Flavor Dried fruit, clove aromas / yeasty flavor, dry finish
Overall Impression Complex and spicy

Reason to Believe Well-respected in the category, Matilda is both a gold and silver medal winner at Great American Beer Festival and World Beer Cup Awards.

MATILDA IS A
tribute to the legend of the abbey where the world-renowned Trappist beer Orval was born. Like the abbey, the beer ages extremely well.

ABV	7.0%
IBU	26
Color	Golden sunrise
Malts	2-Row, Candy Sugar, Caramel
Hops	Golding Celeia, Pilgrim, Saaz, Styrian
Aging	Stainless-aged 3 months; develops in the bottle for up to 5 years
Availability	Year-round; nationwide
Bottling	12-ounce bottle (4-pack)
Draft	1/6 and 1/2 bbl
Preferred Glass	Chalice or Goose Vintage Glassware
Cellaring Notes	Up to 5 years

Taste-Testing
AGED BELGIAN-STYLE ALES

From the farmhouse-style Sofie to our Sour Sisters, each of our Belgian-style ales can be enjoyed immediately or aged for up to five years. The aromas, flavors, and complexity change immensely over time. Like good wine, the qualities of beer depend on the year it was produced, and this is especially true of our Belgian-style beers, which include fresh fruit and wild yeast. What exactly does that mean?

Sometimes even we wonder how the youngest and oldest vintages stack up. In 2016, two of our resident experts, a Sofie brewer and another Sofie expert at the brewery, put a 2010 to 2016 vertical of Sofie to a taste test. This transcript is from that tasting.

THE PROCESS "Sofie is a very unique beer," explains our Sofie brewer. "We do primary fermentation here at the brewery and put the beer in wine barrels with a lot of orange zest and *Brettanomyces* [wild yeast]. We age that first batch of Sofie for about three months. Then, we make a fresh batch and blend that with the aged batch for complexity. At that point, we put Brett yeast in each bottle, so Sofie continues to develop over time."

2010 Vintage

Goose Brewer: Super cloudy. Really great flavor. Wow. Super dry as well, interesting. We're smelling a lot of Brett development over time, the earthy funkiness but none of the bad side that can develop. Brett is an oxygen scavenger. The rate [at which] the yeast consumes the oxygen is what affects the beer's development. The amount of oxygen present in the bottle in the first place can really affect how the beer ages over time.

Resident Sofie Expert: Terrific smell. I'd wear that as perfume. You get all of the oils from the orange peel. And it's so peppery. Really great.

2011

Goose Brewer: The aroma on this is a little more of the barnyard hay character with some vanilla. Not as much citrus as the 2010. I think that might be that some of the richness of the Brett, the "man perfume" you were talking about, is developed more in the 2010. As you get to these older bottles, you get really different characteristics in each.

Resident Sofie Expert: Great flavor, too. Again. This beer holds up really well. You can see it in the older versions.

2012

Goose Brewer: Now we get almost a crystal clear pour. And this is super Brett-y. I also get more tartness out of this. It's still dry, but more acidic.

Resident Sofie Expert: Horse blanket. That's what I get. But in a good way. The Brett is creating its own little universe here.

2013

Goose Brewer: I love this year. It's the year I started working at Goose. This beer is completely different. You can really detect the changes. Definitely oxidized with papery aromas.

Resident Sofie Expert: All of that, yes. And it's a lot more round, with fruits like raisin and dried fig. And then the dryness on top of that.

2014

Goose Brewer: Interesting. A hint of oak in this one, that's the first time I've tasted it distinctly. Everything is starting to really develop.

Resident Sofie Expert: And this one is dry. You can really detect the fresh orange and barrel flavors. It doesn't have the same complex flavors of the older bottles, but you can tell it's really starting to go over that hill. Right in between the freshness and the aged.

2015

Goose Brewer: This is hazier. That smells awesome. Sofie at a year or two has always been among my favorite vintages. That bright orange character balances a little of that mushroomy earthy character of the Brett.

Resident Sofie Expert: I get a little more of the tannin off the barrels here, too, that character.

2016

Goose Brewer: This is a completely different beer. This was just bottled a few days ago. The Brett has done very little so far, maybe a little vanilla. Not nearly as dry, either. There is a lot going on in this beer. The flavors are all there, they are all over the place. It's a very good beer, even now. I think in three months, even six months, you can really tell they will get more formality.

Resident Sofie Expert: I really get the fresh hops, they are so well balanced. Nice and grassy. The barrel is right there, too.

THE SOUR SISTERS
Brewed for food

Fruity, sour ales trace their roots to Belgian Lambics, a style brewed by using airborne yeast to create spontaneous fermentation, a notoriously challenging process. Lambic yeast hails from the Senne River Valley in Belgium, where the environment has long been perfect for these naturally occurring yeasts. (Spontaneous fermentation is hardly limited to a single region; it was likely the way ancient Sumerians brewed beer more than five thousand years ago.) Traditional Belgian Lambics are one of the few beer styles still fermented today with truly wild, airborne yeast.

Those airborne yeasts are great to have around if the goal is to produce a wild sour ale. They can also have the opposite effect: spoiling a batch of beer. Even today, when most modern brewers use a cultivated version of wild yeast, *Brettanomyces bruxellensis* (commonly called *Brettanomyces* or Brett for short), the brewing process can go awry. We've all had the dreaded spoiled batch experience at one time or another, especially when the goal is creative experimentation. As one Goose Island brewer explains, "sour ales are a test of both your brewing skill and patience, but the result is incredible."

Peaches, Berries (Strawberry, Raspberry, Blackberry), Cherries, Lemons, Oranges, Grapefruit, Grapes, Sour Plums, Peppercorns, Yeast, Honey, Balsamic Vinegar, Cider, Bread Dough, Oak, Pine, Grass, Earth

Our series of limited-release wild ales are fermented in wine casks with wild yeasts and lightly barrel-aged with bright, seasonal fruits: farm-fresh raspberries, blackberries, strawberries, peaches, or tart cherries. These complex, pleasantly pucker-worthy ales share the underlying qualities distinct to Belgian-style ales brewed with wild yeast.

The Sour Ale Brewing Process

The primary difference between brewing and aging beers like Bourbon County Brand Stout, the Sour Sisters, Matilda, and our other barrel-aged Belgian-style beers is this secondary wild yeast fermentation.

Traditionally, the fruit is added to Belgian Lambics after the beer has barrel aged (in stainless steel tanks or directly to the bottle). With our beers, additional ingredients like fresh fruit are typically added in the wood barrels during that secondary fermentation in the barrel, though there are exceptions. To make Gillian, for example, fresh summer strawberries are added to the barrels during the secondary (Brett) fermentation, in keeping with when the fruit is added to barrels for our other Sour Sisters. Two months later, honey and white peppercorns are introduced to the barrels with champagne yeast so the beer can undergo a third fermentation process.

For more on the brewing and barrel-aging process, see the section starting on page 50.

ANNUAL RELEASE CALENDAR

Lolita February
Halia April
Gillian June
Juliet August
Madame Rose October

INITIAL VINTAGE RELEASE

2005 Matilda, Belgian-style Pale Ale
2009 Sofie and Juliet
2010 Madame Rose, Lolita
2013 Gillian, Halia

STAGE 1
Primary fermentation → Stainless steel tanks + House yeast

STAGE 2
Additions → Fresh fruit/herbs/spices + Wild yeast (a Brett derivative)

STAGE 3
Secondary fermentation → Wine barrels

Aging → 8 to 18 months (3 months for Sofie) in the ideal Chicago climate

STAGE 4
Blending and bottling → After aging, our brewers "rack," or empty, the barrels. After a tasting, the brewmaster then blends each barrel in batches to reflect the best qualities of that year's vintage. The flavor profile is unique to each vintage.

Wine-Like Qualities The Sour Sisters have earned cult-like status among beer aficionados. They also offer an incredible range of layered aromas and flavors that appeals to wine enthusiasts.

Complexity & Vintage Appeal The wine parallels go beyond nuanced aromas and flavors. Like a good wine, the qualities of each beer vary subtly with every vintage; the age of the beer also influences the aroma and flavor profile. While each beer can be enjoyed immediately, all of our Belgian-style ales develop incredible complexity over time. A vertical tasting can be an eye-opening experience—even for brewers and our other resident experts.

Serving Like wine, the Sour Sisters should be served in the proper glassware. A stemmed chalice or our **Goose Vintage Glassware** is ideal to properly release the aromatics. The stem keeps warm hands away from the glass and a medium-size bowl and concave taper hold in complex aromas, while the flare at the lip encourages a foamy head. A snifter, goblet, or red wine glass could be substituted if a chalice is not available (for more on beer glassware, see pages 170–73).

Wait, what size bottle is that? Most wine bottles are 750ml. The Sour Sisters and our other large-format bottled ales like Sofie and Matilda are sold in 765ml bottles. We've heard all kinds of speculation from the beer community about the reason why. The real reason? With a traditional 750ml bottle, the beer level was just beneath the Goose label on the neck of the bottle. Basically, we looked like stingy beer curmudgeons. A custom, bigger bottle solves the problem and means beer lovers get a bonus 15ml of beer in each bottle. It's a bubbly win-win.

Quality Ingredients

As with all of our beers, we source only the best brewing ingredients. With the Sour Sisters, that selection is even more important. The fruit we use is specially selected, harvested, and prepared to brew beer with the quality of a fine wine.

Hops All of the beers in the Sour Sisters series include the Pilgrim hop variety, known for its fruity aroma with berry, citrus (especially lemon), and pear notes. These qualities lend complexity to the existing fresh, fruity flavors in each beer. Similar to the tannins in wine grapes, additional hop varieties provide bitterness to balance the sweeter flavors in each beer.

Fruit Each variety of fruit is carefully selected and harvested at the peak of flavor. Like a winemaker, our brewers tweak each batch of ale depending on the varieties and quality of fruit available. We source our fruit from small family farmers, the same farmers who supply chefs and home cooks at local farmers' markets. All of our fruit hails from the nearby Great Lakes area, and primarily comes from Michigan.

The fruit is processed in several large wine crushers/destemmers to both remove the stems and pits and puree the fruit to the consistency required for brewing. Typically used in winemaking, these machines work exceptionally well for the berries and stone fruit that we use in the Sour Sisters. (For more on the process, see page 102.)

Lolita Raspberries from Michigan farms typically arrive in late June to early July through the early fall. We use a variety of berries, including tangy Preludes, complex Joan J berries, and wine-like Jaclyn raspberries. Each variety hits its flavor peak at a different point in the season.

Halia Our white peaches are typically sourced from Michigan farms in late July and early August. Our brewers especially love Red Havens, a coveted variety that dates to the 1930s with a sweet, luscious true "peach" flavor.

Gillian Strawberries with names like Cabot and Jewel arrive at the brewery in June and July. All are sweet, brightly flavored varieties that grow well in cooler weather (like our other fruit, they hail from nearby northern farms).

Juliet Blackberries are late summer arrivals, typically from August to early September. The Chester and Triple Crowns varieties tend to be sweeter, while Natchez berries are tart and tangy. We blend the varieties available and tweak the recipe to create the optimal flavor profile.

Madame Rose Each July, boxes filled with ripe Montmorency cherries arrive at the Fulton Street Brewery from farms in southwestern Michigan. The tart variety has semi-sweet notes that balance the flavor well.

IN ADDITION to the classic 765ml bottle, beginning in 2017 the 12-ounce bottles of the Sour Sisters became available in 4-packs. These elegant, wine-like bottles are ideal for enjoying individual servings at home or in a restaurant setting and are easily transportable for events and outings.

The original bottle label for Lolita was based on the cover art for the first edition of Nabokov's *Lolita*.

LOLITA
Bracing and juicy—like a good novel

Lolita is aged in oak wine barrels for eight months or longer with fresh raspberries using Belgian "Orval" Clone and *Brettanomyces bruxellensis* yeasts.

Style Belgian-style wild ale
Additions Raspberries
Cooperage Oak neutral wine barrels
Aroma / Flavor Jam, vanilla aromas / bright berry flavor, dry balsamic finish
Overall Impression Tart, bright, and effervescent
Audience Belgian Framboise, Kir Royale, rosé and Nabokov fans

Rating 92/100 Beer Advocate

" **OAK, RED WINE,** *and berry notes waft from the glass, intriguing the drinker. Upon the first taste, the mouth is greeted with a light sweetness that bursts with berry flavor ... [followed by] notes of wine and oaky tannins that slowly fade into pleasant tartness. The sour notes are subdued and held in check by the light sweetness."*

—*Porch Drinking*, November 20, 2013

ABV	(varies) 8.1%
IBU	(varies) 32
Color	Pink rose
Malts	2-Row, Caramel
Hops	Golding Celeia, Pilgrim, Saaz, Styrian
Aging	Barrel-aged for at least 8 months
Availability	Limited release; February to March
Bottling	12-ounce bottle (4-pack)
Draft	1/6 bbl
Preferred Glass	Chalice or Goose Vintage Glassware
Cellaring Notes	Up to 5 years

HALIA
Fresh and delicate—one to remember

Halia is aged in oak wine barrels for up to one year with fresh white peaches using Saison and *Brettanomyces clauseneii* yeasts.

Style Belgian-style farmhouse ale
Additions White peaches
Cooperage Oak neutral wine barrels
Aroma / Flavor Tropical aromas / fresh peach flavor, dry-tart finish
Overall Impression Fresh, delicate, and effervescent
Audience Bellini and Riesling fans

Rating 93/100 Beer Advocate

" **THE PRESENCE OF**
Brett keeps Halia from becoming cloyingly sweet, and the oak from the barrels imparts a density that you'd typically associate with a high-end wine. The finish is crisp and tart, with echoes of a dry white wine mixed with another round of peach."

—Paste Magazine, January 22, 2014

Literally "remembrance of a loved one" in Hawaiian, Halia was created in memory of a brewer's dear friend, who loved peaches.

ABV	(varies) 7.9%
IBU	(varies) 11
Color	Golden
Malts	2-Row, Pilsner, Torrified Wheat
Hops	Amarillo
Aging	Barrel-aged for at least 8 months
Availability	Limited release; April to May
Bottling	12-ounce bottle (4-pack)
Draft	1/6 bbl
Preferred Glass	Chalice or Goose Vintage Glassware
Cellaring Notes	Up to 5 years

Inspired by an amuse-bouche often prepared by the chef wife of one of our brewers, the recipe for Gillian marries the same strawberry, spicy pepper, and honey flavors in the bottle and is the only Sour Sister that uses champagne yeast.

GILLIAN

Bright and complex—a summer night's toast

Gillian is aged in oak wine barrels for two months with fresh strawberries using Saison and *Brettanomyces bruxellensis* yeasts, and then aged an additional three to six months with honey, white peppercorns, and champagne yeast.

Style Belgian-style farmhouse ale
Additions Strawberries, white pepper, honey
Cooperage Oak neutral wine barrels
Aroma / Flavor Peppery, wine-like aromas / earthy, berry flavors, tart finish
Overall Impression Spicy and complex
Audience Belgian Sour and dry rosé wine fans

Rating 92/100 Beer Advocate

> # GILLIAN IS SPRITZY AND EFFERVESCENT,
> *its tart, mouthwatering fruitiness and honeyed sweetness balanced by mineral bitterness and an astringency like grape skin and pine resin…. Strawberry blends with cantaloupe, pomegranate, sumac, and preserved lemon peel, all of it atop toasted almond, water cracker, and tannins and vanilla from the oak."*
>
> —*Chicago Reader*, October 21, 2014

GILLIAN WAS NAMED AFTER

actress Gillian Anderson, who worked as a hostess at Goose Island's Clybourn Brewpub in 1988. The beer was originally called "Scully."

ABV	(varies) 8.5%
IBU	(varies) 11
Color	Hazy, rosy sunset
Malts	2-Row, Pilsner, Torrified Wheat
Hops	Zythos
Aging	Barrel-aged for 5 to 8 months
Availability	Limited release; June to July
Bottling	12-ounce bottle (4-pack)
Preferred Glass	Chalice or Goose Vintage Glassware
Cellaring Notes	Up to 5 years

JULIET
Tart, jammy, and nuanced—a trip to wine country

Aged in oak wine barrels for up to one year with blackberries using House Ale and *Brettanomyces bruxellensis* yeasts.

Style Belgian-style wild ale
Additions Blackberries
Cooperage Oak neutral wine barrels
Aroma / Flavor Berry, woodsy aromas / tart, dark fruit flavor, earthy finish
Overall Impression Tart, fruity, and complex
Audience Belgian Sour and Old World Pinot Noir fans

Rating 95/100 Beer Advocate

Our homage to a gracious host on many travels to Belgium, Juliet was named after the sister of the owner and a fourth-generation brewer of Cantillon.

ABV	(varies) 8.2%
IBU	(varies) 11
Color	Burgundy
Malts	Special Pale Ale, Rye, Munich
Hops	Pilgrim
Aging	Barrel-aged for 12 months
Availability	Limited release; August to September
Bottling	12-ounce bottle (4-pack)
Draft	1/6 bbl
Preferred Glass	Chalice or Goose Vintage Glassware
Cellaring Notes	Up to 5 years

"**JULIET MIXES** *several beer traits such as caramel malt and Belgian yeast with multiple wine traits such as fruit, higher alcohol, oak, and tannins, then spikes the cocktail with a moderate dose of souring and a light touch of* Brettanomyces *funk to produce a complex and tasty drinking experience.*"

—SourBeerBlog.com, July 26, 2014

Belgium's first female brewmaster, Rosa Blancquaert-Merck, was the former brewery manager of the historical Liefmans brewery. Rosa was dedicated to brewing beers using the traditional methods of the region. Rosa's passion for the tradition of brewing at Liefmans and her desire to share the Oud Bruin style of beer with the world became an inspiration to the Goose Island brewers. Madame Rose is named in her honor.

MADAME ROSE
Alluring and earthy—a rose by any other name

Madame Rose is aged in oak cabernet wine barrels for up to eighteen months with fresh, tart Michigan cherries using House Ale followed by multiple yeast strains.

Style Belgian-style wild ale (Oud Bruin)
Additions Cherries
Cooperage Oak neutral wine barrels
Aroma / Flavor Woody, leather aromas / earthy, tart cherry and spice flavors
Overall Impression Tart, dry, and complex
Audience Belgian Kriek and Bordeaux wine fans

"IT'S THE COLOR OF

a well-made Manhattan cocktail, a hazy, red/orange/rusty brown, and raises a thin collar of foam. The aroma is riotous—sour fruit, acetic acid, and a barn's worth of horsey Brett. The palate shows and electric acidity balanced against austere sweetness, a burst of dark fruit and balsamic vinegar in the center and a linear finish that only lifts its foot off the pedal at the last second."

—*All About Beer*, September 16, 2014
(Garrett Oliver, brewmaster, Brooklyn Brewery)

OUD BRUIN
means "old brown" or "old ales" and refers to the beers traditionally brewed in western Flanders. A handful of breweries that produce these beers, like Liefmans, have been in the area since the 1600s. The higher-alcohol, sour style, known as a "provision beer," emerged as a beer that aged and traveled well on long ship journeys. Traditional Flanders versions were aged in oak vessels. The result was a beer with bright, fruity-sour notes and incredible complexity.

THE ROSELARRE
yeast blend used during secondary fermentation, or while the beer is barrel aging, is a mix of five lambic cultures: *Brettanomyces bruxellensis* and *lambicus* (a sherry strain), and two lactic acid–producing bacteria (*Pediococcus* and *Lactobacillus*). Together they lend a complex, earthy, and cherry pie-like sourness typical of the Oud Bruin beers of Belgium.

ABV	(varies) 6.7%
IBU	(varies) 12
Color	Deep crimson
Malts	2-Row, Wheat, CaraPils, Special B, Chocolate
Hops	Pilgrim Yeast House Ale (primary), Roselarre blend (secondary)
Aging	Barrel-aged for up to 18 months
Availability	Limited release; October to November
Bottling	12-ounce bottle (4-pack)
Draft	1/6 bbl
Preferred Glass	Chalice or Goose Vintage Glassware
Cellaring Notes	Up to 5 years

BOURBON COUNTY BRAND STOUT
The first of its kind

In the early 1990s, Goose Island pioneered the process of aging beers in freshly emptied bourbon barrels when brewmaster Greg Hall famously received a gift of barrels from former Jim Beam Master Distiller Booker Noe. Brewed in honor of our thousandth batch of beer, the inaugural beer in the Bourbon County Brand Stout series was dark, mysterious, and certainly unforgettable.

That single release helped shape an entirely new generation of barrel-aged beers that followed, both at Goose Island and beyond. For more on the launch of the Bourbon County Brand Stout series, see page 26.

Each release is unique yet maintains the unsurpassable quality that has made the Bourbon County Brand Stout series a cult beer.

Today, our Bourbon County Brand Stout series includes four core brands: **Original**, **Coffee**, **Proprietor's**, and **Barleywine**, with special releases available in select years. Each and every batch adheres to our time-honored brewing practices and, most importantly, the aging process.

For nearly a year, the stout soaks up the flavors in eight- to twelve-year-old bourbon barrels (see The Barrel-Aging Process, pages 76–79). Each barrel is used only once, providing an unparalleled complexity in every bottle. Special releases like the Bourbon County Reserve Brand Barleywine, which is aged in 2015 Bourbon County Brand Rare barrels, are among the few exceptions (see page 121).

Smoke, Tobacco, Charred Oak, Maple, Chocolate, Vanilla, Caramel, Roasted Coffee Beans, Cocoa Nibs, Coconut, Caramel, Brown Sugar, Cinnamon, Star Anise, Toasted Pecans, Chipotle Peppers, Peppercorns, Blackberries, Sour Cherries

All of our Bourbon County Brand Stout beers are produced in limited quantities. They are released the fourth Friday of November at our Black Friday release (see page 118).

Bourbon County Brand Stout
Bourbon County Brand Coffee Stout
Bourbon County Brand Proprietor's Blend (Chicago release only)
Bourbon County Brand Barleywine
Bourbon County Brand Special Releases

Style Barrel-aged stout
Additions Varies
Cooperage Oak bourbon, rye, or other liquor-aged wood barrels
Aroma / Flavor Varies; typically with chocolate and earthy notes
Overall Impression Bold, rich, and complex
Audience Cult beer and fine liquor fans

Since 2015, all of the Goose Island Bourbon County Brand Stout beers have been released in custom-designed, 16.9-ounce bottles.

Black FRIDAY

The beers in our Bourbon County Brand Stout series are released on one day a year: Black Friday, otherwise known as the day after Thanksgiving. It started as a way to make the beer we love so much available to devoted fans on a low-key day after the holidays.

Soon, the event took on a life—and line—of its own. Each year, loyal Bourbon County Brand Stout fans line up outside a designated local liquor store in time for the doors to open at 9 a.m. Bourbon County loyalists line up early ... very early.

Coffee and doughnuts have become a staple offering of encouragement (and warmth) for those who spent Thanksgiving night braving the Chicago winter weather as they camped on the street. Goose employees have even delivered a Thanksgiving dinner to one of the beer's most loyal devotees, who often lines up on the Wednesday prior to the release—all for the chance to buy two bottles of the original Bourbon County Brand Stout and one bottle of each of our other offerings that year.

Some might call them crazy. We just call them people who know a good beer when they taste one.

BOURBON COUNTY ON TAP

On Black Friday, our Fulton Street Brewpub offers timed draft tastings of the newest Bourbon County Brand releases all day long. Check the website for times each beer will be available. Special flight tastings and other special offerings may require advance tickets.

Clybourn Avenue will also continue to offer special promotions related to Bourbon County Brand Stout on Black Friday.

Anniversary
CELEBRATION

In 2017, Knob Creek, the straight bourbon that Booker Noe created, celebrated its twenty-fifth anniversary. We were proud to commemorate our shared B&Bs—beer and bourbon—milestones with an equally special release: Bourbon County Reserve Brand Stout aged in retired Knob Creek barrels.

This special edition release is complemented by one of the best Bourbon County lineups ever. Bourbon County Brand Original, Barleywine, Coffee, Northwoods (Blueberry Almond), and Proprietor's (this year, 2017, inspired by bananas foster).

To round out a very special year, are also brewing and aging Bourbon County Reserve Brand Barleywine. It is made with Bourbon County Barleywine aged in our 2015 Bourbon County Brand Rare barrels. From Heaven Hill Distilleries, these American white oak barrels were originally used to age bourbon for more than thirty years before being used to age our 2015 Bourbon County Rare.

> 🌿 The Bourbon County Reserve Brand Stout is being aged in Booker's retired Knob Creek barrels that we procured from the distillery.

The Art & Science of

BARREL AGING BEER

Have you had a beer recently? Probably. But what about a beer aged in bourbon barrels? Learn more about the calculated steps, time, and thoughtful care that goes into producing the deep character of your barrel-aged stout.

— PHASE 1 —

Goose Island Bourbon County Brand Stout

WHERE BOURBON COMES FROM

To be classified "Bourbon" it has to be distilled in the United States, 51% corn in the mash bill and be put into a brand new charred American white oak barrel.

51%

Bourbon barrels are made from **AMERICAN WHITE OAK TREES**

The spirit goes into the barrel crystal-clear. **CHARRING THE BARREL AND CARAMELIZING THE WOOD SUGARS** lends the spirit its color and flavor as it ages

---

— PHASE 2 —

Goose Island Bourbon County Brand Stout

BREWING PROCESS

MASH TUN

Hot water and a blend of malts make a sweet slurry with the consistency of porridge.

 Goose Island's Russian Imperial Stout uses **SIX DIFFERENT MALTS WEIGHING ABOUT 5,000 LBS** for each brew.

LAUTER TUN

Brewers then separate the grain solids from the liquid, called sweet wort.

BREW KETTLE

In order to sterilize, stabilize and concentrate sugar in beer:

 Wort needs to be brought to a boil for at least **60 MINUTES**.

 12 LBS OF HOPS are added to each brew.

 Bourbon County Brand Stout will see **A 3-4 HOUR BOIL** to concentrate sugars.

COOLING

For fermentation to take place, the yeast must cool down.

 A heat exchanger cools down the hot wort using **COLD CITY WATER.**

62° The target temperature is **62 DEGREES FAHRENHEIT** for Bourbon County Brand Stout.

FERMENTATION

Chilled wort is pumped into a fermentation tank with 100 gallons of yeast, which produces CO2, alcohol, heat, aroma, and flavor to Bourbon County Brand Stout.

— PHASE 3 —
Goose Island Bourbon County Brand Stout
AGING PROCESS

Post fermentation, the Russian Imperial Stout is pumped into freshly emptied bourbon barrels stored for the next 8-12 months to extract color, flavor, and aroma.

GOOSE ISLAND'S BARREL HOUSE IS LOCATED IN CHICAGO, a city with extreme temperatures throughout the year (hot summers, cold winters), which has a great impact on the aging process.

DURING HOT CHICAGO SUMMERS, the warm temperatures cause wood to expand, allowing the beer to penetrate deep into the wood pores.

 WOOD ALLOWS LIQUID TO EVAPORATE from the barrel, making the beer richer and more concentrated.

 THE TERM "ANGEL'S SHARE" is used to describe the lost volume due to evaporation during the aging process.

 THE TERM "DEVIL'S CUT" is used to describe the lost volume due to beer being absorbed deep into the barrel staves.

COLD TEMPERATURES cause wood to contract, squeezing beer out of the wood pores and back into the contents of the barrel, bringing with it the character of the bourbon.

— PHASE 4 —
Goose Island Bourbon County Brand Stout
PACKAGING

After the 8-12 months of this Russian Imperial Stout aging, the brewers racket the bourbon barrels. "Racking" is the term for emptying a cask.

EACH BARREL IS BLENDED TOGETHER in batches that reflect the best tasting blend of the barrel-aged beer. Once that happens it is ready to be packaged.

To ensure Bourbon County Stout has as much time as it can in the barrel, **GOOSE ISLAND EMPTIES THEM AS LATE AS POSSIBLE** to meet the Black Friday release date. This could be only a few weeks!

— PHASE 5 —
Goose Island Bourbon County Brand Stout
FINISHED PRODUCT & FLAVOR PROFILE

The dynamic Chicago weather that causes the expansion and contraction of the wood creates a Bourbon County Brand Stout that is unique year to year.

This complex profile is comprised of different flavors from the **BOURBON BARREL'S VARIOUS LAYERS.**

CHAR LAYER
Smoke, chocolate, and roasted coffee

BOURBON LAYER
Coconut, caramel, vanilla and cherry

ABSORPTION LAYER
Tobacco and leather

RAW WOOD LAYER
Earthy and woody

BOURBON COUNTY BRAND STOUT

The tried-and-true original. The nose is an intense mix of charred oak, chocolate, vanilla, caramel, and smoke, with wine-like variances in every vintage.

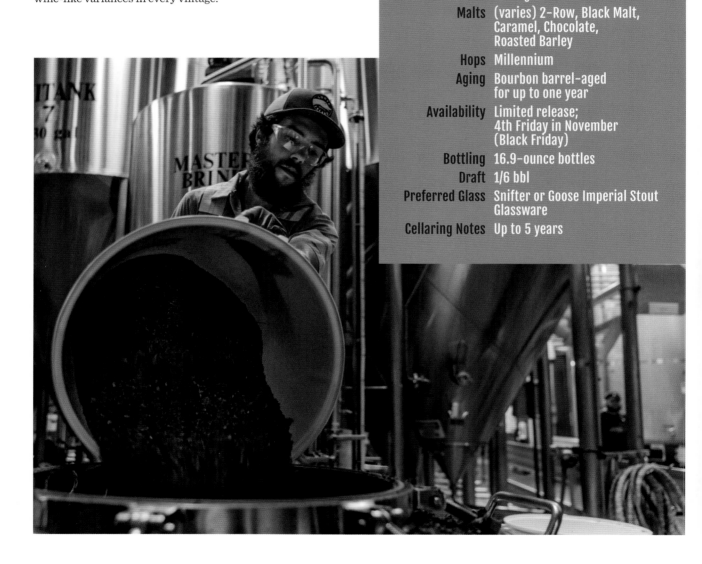

ABV	(varies) 12% and above
IBU	(varies) 60
Color	Midnight black
Malts	(varies) 2-Row, Black Malt, Caramel, Chocolate, Roasted Barley
Hops	Millennium
Aging	Bourbon barrel-aged for up to one year
Availability	Limited release; 4th Friday in November (Black Friday)
Bottling	16.9-ounce bottles
Draft	1/6 bbl
Preferred Glass	Snifter or Goose Imperial Stout Glassware
Cellaring Notes	Up to 5 years

BOURBON COUNTY BRAND COFFEE STOUT

Every day, Goose Island brewers smell Intelligentsia's coffee literally roasting in their facilities next to the brewery. (We drink a lot of really good coffee around here.) Our coffee stout is made with a different bean variety each year, chosen in collaboration with our brewers and Intelligentsia's world-class coffee experts.

The aromas and flavors of each vintage vary based on the flavor profile of the coffee beans selected and how our brewers choose to highlight the flavors. The coffee bean variety's name is listed on each bottle.

ABV	(varies) 12.5%
IBU	(varies) 60
Color	Midnight black
Malts	(varies) 2-Row, Black Malt, Munich, Chocolate, Caramel, Roasted Barley, Black Malt
Hops	(varies) Millennium, Columbus, Willamette
Aging	Bourbon barrel–aged for up to 1 year
Availability	Limited release; 4th Friday in November (Black Friday)
Bottling	16.9-ounce bottles (12-ounce bottles for 2014 and earlier vintages)
Draft	1/6 bbl
Preferred Glass	Snifter or Goose Imperial Stout Glassware
Cellaring Notes	Up to 5 years

GETTING THE COFFEE FLAVOR INTO THE BEER

There are many different ways to add coffee and its aromas and flavors to beer. We could add whole or ground beans, or even brewed coffee, directly to the boil, or put those coffee beans or brewed coffee into the fermenter. With a barrel-aged beer, the coffee can also be put into the barrel to age with the stout.

The method that worked best for Goose Island and Intelligentsia, in terms of maintaining both the integrity of the beer and the coffee, was to mix cold-brewed coffee (one that has been steeped for twenty-four hours without heat and then pressed, producing a less acidic and sweeter-tasting coffee than conventionally brewed coffee) with the finished Bourbon County Stout at the bottling stage.

2016 Intelligentsia Fletcha Roja (Costa Rica)
Bean qualities: stone fruit (cherry), chocolate, toasted nuts

2015 Intelligentsia Los Delirios (Nicaragua)
Bean qualities: caramel, vanilla, orange

2014 Intelligentsia Zirikana (Rwanda)
Bean qualities: apple, almond, sweet herbs

2013 Intelligentsia Los Inmortales (El Salvador)
Bean qualities: smoke, chocolate

2012 Intelligentsia La Tortuga (Honduras)
Bean qualities: tobacco, wood

2011 Intelligentsia Anjilanaka (Bolivia)
Bean qualities: floral, pear, honey

2010 Intelligentsia Black Cat Espresso (Brazil, Costa Rica)
Bean qualities: caramel, chocolate, stone fruit (peach)

PROPRIETOR'S BOURBON COUNTY BRAND STOUT

Launched in 2013, our most experimental in the Bourbon County series is an annual vintage brewed in honor of Chicago—and only for Chicago-area release. We brew our Proprietor's Blend to show our immense gratitude for our neighbors, those loyal and adventurous fans whose support helped bring the original Bourbon County Brand Stout to towering heights.

Bananas and pecans? Roasted marshmallows? Curry powder? Each year, a combination of unique ingredients is chosen to add to the stout before it's aged. Choosing the right type of barrel to maximize the flavor profile is also a key part of the process. The recipe is the winner of an internal brewer's competition. (A half dozen Bourbon County Brand Stout bottles to taste and tinker around with at home? Yes, please.)

2016
Additional Ingredients: chipotle peppers, cocoa nibs
Aging: bourbon barrels that previously stored maple syrup
Originator: Goose Island brewer Emily Kosmal

2015
Additional Ingredients: maple, toasted pecans, guajillo peppers
Aging: bourbon barrels
Originator: Goose Island brewer Diana "Di" Rodriguez

2014
Additional Ingredients: cassia bark, cocoa nibs, coconut water
Aging: rye barrels
Originator: Goose Island brewer Zach Greenwood

2013
Additional Ingredient: toasted coconut
Aging: rye barrels
Originator: Recipe development was a Goose Island team effort. The final recipe was brewed by brewmaster Brett Porter and brewing innovation manager Mike Siegel.

ABV	(varies) 13% and above
IBU	60
Color	Midnight black
Malts	(varies) 2-Row, Black Malt, Munich, Chocolate, Caramel, Roasted Barley, Black Malt
Hops	(varies) Millennium, Columbus, Willamette
Aging	Barrel-aged (various barrels) up to 1 year
Availability	Chicago only; 4th Friday in November (Black Friday)
Bottling	16.9-ounce bottles (12- and 22-ounce bottles for 2014 and earlier vintages)
Draft	1/6 bbl
Preferred Glass	Snifter or Goose Imperial Stout Glassware
Cellaring Notes	Up to 5 years

BOURBON COUNTY BRAND BARLEYWINE

Aged in the third-use barrels that were once home to Kentucky bourbon and then to our Bourbon County Brand Stout, this traditional English-style barleywine possesses the subtlety of flavor that only comes from a barrel that has gone through many seasons of ritual care.

The intricacies of the previous barrel denizens—oak, charcoal, hints of tobacco and vanilla, and that signature bourbon heat—are all present in this beer. Hearty and complex, Bourbon County Brand Barleywine is a titan and a timeline, a bold, flavorful journey through the craft of barrel aging.

BARLEYWINE IS A TRADITIONAL ENGLISH ALE

brewed at higher temperatures and aged to produce a complex, richly flavored, and often higher-alcohol beer. The aging process produced a beer with more complexity. Descendants of the traditional style include English and American hybrids, which tend to exemplify the rich complexity of the style. Our Bourbon County Brand Barleywine is unique in that it is aged in bourbon barrels.

ABV	(varies) 13.6%
IBU	60
Color	Deep crimson
Malts	(varies) 2-Row, Munich, Chocolate, Roast Barley, Black Malt
Hops	Millennium
Aging	Barrel-aged for up to 1 year
Availability	Limited Release; 4th Friday in November (Black Friday)
Bottling	16.9-ounce bottles
Draft	⅙ bbl
Preferred Glass	Snifter or Goose Imperial Stout Glassware
Cellaring Notes	Up to 5 years

SINGLE VINTAGE BOURBON COUNTY BRAND STOUT

Our brewers create unique Bourbon County Brand releases when the inspiration strikes and the barrel stars align. The following beers are a few fine examples of this evolving category. Each is available in very limited quantities.

Bourbon County Regal Rye, 2015

Our rye barrel–aging experiments began as a natural offshoot of our bourbon barrel–aging program. In 2013, our brewers experimented with a Backyard Rye aged with mulberries, boysenberries, and marionberries.

Developed by the team of Goose Island brewers, the 2015 Regal Rye was particularly collaborative. The brewers submitted recipes, held a roundtable discussion dissecting each, and in the end landed on this winning recipe. Blackberries, Luxardo candied cherries, fresh sour cherries, and sea salt were aged with Bourbon County Brand Stout in rye whiskey barrels. The brew received a 96/100 rating on Beer Advocate.

Bourbon County Rare, 2015

Back in 1979, the folks at Heaven Hill Distilleries filled a handful of new, freshly charred American white oak barrels with some of their finest whiskey. The spirit was left to patiently age for over thirty years (more than twenty-three years is rare). In that time, both the bourbon and the barrels developed a distinct, truly one-of-a-kind character. We were lucky enough to procure the barrels. We filled these very special barrels with Bourbon County Brand Stout, and then tucked them away in our Chicago Barrel Warehouse to age for two more years. Our brewers believe this is one of the finest beers we have ever produced.

Bourbon County Rare Barleywine, 2017

The barrels from Heaven Hill Distilleries that were used to age whiskey for more than thirty years, and later Bourbon County Rare (above), were reused again. This time, our barleywine went into the barrels for a layered complexity like none we have tasted in a barleywine.

FULTON & WOOD
At the intersection of brewing & innovation

We believe a well-crafted brewing program values both tradition and change, and the Fulton & Wood series is the intersection of these ideals. Even the name is a tribute. Located at the corner of Fulton & Wood streets in Chicago, Goose Island's original brewery has been a hub of innovation since its doors opened.

Each release in the Fulton & Wood series gives Goose Island employees from throughout the company the chance to work with our brewers not only to dream up a new beer, but to actually create one. Some of our most adventurous and inspired beers have come from teams of people from all over the company: brewers, accountants, marketers, operations. Everyone.

For more on the Fulton & Wood story, see page 49.

In 2017, we expanded the program further. The four bottled releases of our most popular past Fulton & Wood releases: Fassinator (February), My Shout (May), Dark Traveler (August), and 1516 (November) were accompanied by four Chicago area–only draft releases. The draft releases were released seasonally, and included a cream ale, a grissette, a pear sour, and an Irish stout.

IN 2016, for the first time, Goose Island debuted a series of four Fulton & Wood bottled beers featuring the most successful recent experiments as well as favorites from years past. A new bottled offering was offered seasonally to select markets.

Select Fulton & Wood Releases

The beers released nationwide in our Fulton & Wood series vary annually. Here are a few of our recent favorites.

C.A.L.M. Radler German-style Radler
A radler is the German equivalent of a beer cocktail. Beer and sparkling lemonade were mixed to created a light, refreshing drink that dates to the early twentieth century. It was supposedly meant to fuel thirsty cyclists passing through town when an innkeeper's beer supply was running low (the radler is cousin to the British shandy). Our version starts as a wheat ale with a light and crisp flavor and a creamy, smooth body. The ale is then blended with a sparkling lime soda with cucumber and fresh mint to create a refreshing summer radler. Ride on.

Rasselbock "Dunkelroggenweizenbock"
Goose Island lead cellarman and former brewer Patrick Reisch and his team worked to combine the elements of a doppelbock (a strong lager), roggenbier (rye beer), and a Bavarian weiss (wheat beer), creating a beer with clove aromatics, a hint of banana, and a dry rye finish. The team worked to find the perfect balance of grains so Rasselbock is more than just a Frankenstein of beer styles; it evokes a German-style wheat and rye beer all in one. The creamy body and frothy head are as thick as the fever dream most likely responsible for its invention, and the subtle spice note comes from the Weihenstephan yeast, a familiar strain from brewer Patrick's internship experience at Spaten-Franziskaner-Bräu in Germany. It's the perfect beer for that mashup of seasons as winter slowly turns into spring.

Fassinator Blonde Doppelbock
"Fahss-in-ator," as Arnold Schwarzenegger would say, is Goose Island's take on a blonde doppelbock. The name is derived from the combination of the German word for "on draught," *vom Faß*, and the traditional suffix of many doppelbocks, which is *-ator*. Fassinator has a subtle hop aroma with a moderate body, a smooth biscuit malt flavor, and moderate bitterness, creating a unique balance for this

classic style. Don't underestimate the chops behind this beer; Fassinator clocks in at a hefty 8.0% ABV. *Hasta la vista*, baby.

My Shout Australian-style sparkling ale
Named for an Australian way of calling out for the next round of beers, My Shout brings a style that has rarely been seen in the US to Chicago. Brewed with an Australian sparkling ale yeast, hints of apricot and stone fruit combined with mild but spicy and citrusy hops make My Shout a refreshing way to forget about the subzero temperatures and take a 16-ounce trip to summer Down Under. G'day, Chicago.

Dark Traveler Munich Dunkel
Bridging the gap between the Old World and New World, the Dark Traveler brings back a little-known beer style: the Munich Dunkel. The famous brown lager developed in part due to the city's slightly carbonated water supply and later became popular throughout Bavaria. The Fulton & Wood team behind this beer used American and Czech hops, three different kinds of wheat, and Belgian oats, all while carefully replicating the profile of the Munich classic. Our version pours a dark mahogany color and is rich with deep, toasty bread and subtle nutty flavors.

1516 Bavarian Kellerbier
Brewed to honor traditional German brewing practices, 1516 is a gently smoked Bavarian Kellerbier. The beer was named in honor of the 500th anniversary of the German Purity Law, or Reinheitsgebot, of 1516 that stated only water, barley, and hops could be used in the production of beer. Our ale's subtle smokiness, bready-malty notes, and clean finish are both balanced and complex, making it a great beer to drink alone or, even better, with freshly baked pretzels (see Umami in Beer, page 186). Prost!

Bee Squad Bière de Miel
A 400-year-old beer style that was once popular in Belgium and France, Bière de Miel ales are brewed with honey and spices balanced by moderate hops. The style virtually vanished in the 1950s, though it persisted with home brewers (something Goose Island employees have been and still are proud to be). In this updated classic, a Saison-like base is combined with honey and apricot essences and low hopping, yet remains refreshing and light for the ABV (8%). The name was inspired by the brewers as well as by the style. We make beer around the clock at the brewery, with teams of brewers splitting shifts. Every brewer on Bee Squad's team happens to be on the "B" brewing shift, so they call themselves the B Squad.

Casimir Polish-style smoked wheat ale
Chicago has the largest Polish population outside of Warsaw. When three Goose Island brewers (Mike Siegel, Brian Davis, and Jason Karras) learned they each had Polish heritage, they teamed up in 2012 to make a beer inspired by Polish smoked wheat ales. They started by smoking their own wheat with old Bourbon County Brand Stout barrel staves thanks to the generosity of Chicago's Hagen Fish Market, which allowed them to use their smoker. Rye malt (a rye bread inspiration), caraway seeds, and Polish Lublin hops rounded out the mix for this draft-only, truly Chicago-inspired release.

CASIMIR ALE was named after a local hero famous for saving George Washington's life during the revolutionary war. After being recruited by General Washington, Casimir Pulaski spent his life on the battlefields of the northern and southeastern United States and was buried at sea. Even though Casimir reportedly never set foot in Illinois, the state instituted a local holiday on the first Monday in March in the Polish war hero's honor. If you grew up in Chicago, that meant one thing: no school! Now there's a true local hero to Chicago schoolchildren everywhere.

OUR NEW barrel-aged beers deserve a bottle as interesting as the beer inside. In a tribute to the city, each Cooper Project bottle has a Chicago star detail as well as crisp lines that allude to the city's architectural skyline. With a shorter neck and wider body, this is a bottle for a serious beer.

GOOSE ISLAND
COOPER
PROJECT

STYLE:
BARREL-AGED
SCOTCH ALE

COOPERAGE:
BOURBON BARRELS

AGED | 4 MONTHS
20 | 17

RELEASE:
No.1

12 FL. OZ. (355ML) ★ ★ ★ ★   GOOSE ISLAND BEER CO, CHICAGO, IL

BARRELHOUSE SERIES

We have more than a quarter of a century of barrel aging experience under our brewing belts, along with a top-quality barrel-aging warehouse (see page 50). In the years to come, Goose Island will continue to apply that expertise to offer even more top-quality barrel-aged beers.

The Cooper Project

Launched in 2017, the Cooper Project is a rotating series highlighting our expertise in bourbon barrel aging with three new releases each year (one every four months).

2017 Cooper Project Releases

Barrel-Aged Scotch Ale Nicknamed "Wee Heavy," Scotch ale is a full-bodied beer style that was popular in Scotland in the nineteenth century. Typical characteristics include toasted malt and caramel notes and balanced bitterness. Our first Cooper Project release of 2017, aged for four months in bourbon barrels, has notes of rich toffee and roasted malt for a seamless blend of beer and barrel flavors. Release date: February 2017

Barrel-Aged Blonde Doppelbock The "liquid bread" of Bavarian monasteries, doppelbocks take on various food-friendly flavors (toasted bread and nuttiness are typical). They tend to be stronger than other German-style bocks, thus the name "doppel," or double, yet in blonde versions rely on lighter Pils or Vienna malts. Release date: June 2017

Barrel-Aged Porter Barrel-aged stouts put Goose Island on the map; this beer is a tribute to the historical precursor to stout, the porter. We've brewed several porters over the years (Old Clybourn Porter, Baltic Porter, and more) and even experimented with a few barrel-aged versions (2015 Holiday Porter, a Chicago area–only draft release), but this is our first bottled release. Fall and winter are the perfect time to enjoy the roasty, toasty flavors. Release date: October 2017

As a callback to the Bourbon County Brand Stout bottles, a flag on the neck of any Goose Island beer bottle signifies that the beer was aged in bourbon barrels.

ABV	(varies) 7.7%
IBU	24
Color	Deep copper
Malts	2-Row, Special Pale, Bonlander Munich, Crystal Rye, Crystal II, C40, Roast Barley
Hops	East Kent Golding, Northern Brewer
Aging	Bourbon barrel–aged for 4 months
Availability	Select markets

THE FOUDRE PROJECT

The Foudre Project is a series of limited-release beers aged at our barrel-aging warehouse in oak foudres, large wooden vats traditionally used to age wine. Foudres are much larger than oak barrels. Ours were sourced from France and were previously used to house Bordeaux or other French wines.

2017 Foudre Project Releases

Wild Red Ale Inspired by an indigenous beer of West Flanders, these sour ales have wine-like characteristics with a variety of fruit flavors. The first release is aged in foudres for six months and then aged in bourbon barrels for twelve months. This combination of cooperages results in dark, tart cherry and caramel notes with a faint vanilla backbone. The balanced tartness plays off lemon and citric acidity on the nose and a clean, tannic dryness. Release date: January 2017

Future Foudre Project releases will be determined by our brewers.

WHAT THE F

is a Foudre? Foudres (pronounced *FOO-der* and spelled "foudre" in French or "foeder" in Dutch) are essentially giant, upright wooden barrels. The beauty of foudres is that the beer actually undergoes primary fermentation inside the wooden tank (most barrel-aged beer is fully fermented before it is put into the barrel). Unlike with bourbon barrels, our brewers aren't looking for the wooden qualities of foudres; because the foudres are so large, very little of the liquid inside is in contact with the wood. Instead, they are looking for the tiny, beer-friendly bugs that give beer styles like Flanders Red and Oud Bruin their characteristic sour funk and incredible deliciousness.

EXPERIMENTAL

The word "experimental" is always floating around at Goose Island, but this beer portfolio takes that to a wholly different place: a historical beer style that hasn't been brewed in ages, a grunge-rock collaboration with a local Chicago band, and a new riff on a beer style driven solely by curiosity.

We brew these beers knowing that we may never be able to justify the time and expense required to brew some of them again. Alternative, radical, unconventional, avant-garde, experimental ... call it whatever you want. Ultimately, it's what art—and brewing—is all about.

Pitchfork Music Festival Collaboration Beers

Since 2013, the brewery has collaborated with a local band to release a special beer for the Pitchfork Music Festival, an annual three-day summer music celebration in Chicago's Union Park featuring more than forty bands. Beyond the festival in mid-July, these beers are usually available on draft at the Fulton Street Brewpub and at some Chicago-area bars around the same time.

2016 Natural Villain with garage rock band Twin Peaks
A pale lager inspired by some of the band's favorite beers (Modelo, Pacifico, and Sol) and named after their album by the same name.

2015 No Collar with Chance the Rapper
A Helles-style lager for "the hardworking people of Chicago," as Chance the Rapper described it.

2014 SVE with singer-songwriter Sharon von Etten
A refreshing, sessionable (lower-alcohol) Kölsch is a festival-worthy beer that could be sipped all day.

2013 Run the Jewels by rappers Killer Mike and EL-P
A dry-hopped Belgian wheat ale brewed to elicit hints of a certain smokable "cousin to hops" aroma named after the rappers' album by the same name.

Other Projects

The level of brewing curiosity is always high at Goose Island. These beers are the passion projects that our brewers just can't get out of their minds ... and ours. All are limited-release beers, whether available from only a handful of local tap handles or bottled in small quantities to reach beer history buffs overseas.

Brewery Yard Stock Ale

When Mike Siegel, Goose Island's brewing innovation manager, thought it would be fun to revive a long-forgotten, barrel-aged British ale style, he called up British brewing historian Ron Pattison.

As luck would have it, Ron had been trying for years to convince a brewery to make a stock pale ale, a barrel-aged specialty of Burton upon Trent brewers that disappeared after the First World War. The barrel-aged pale ale was known for the amount of hops used—up to five times as much as an Imperial or double IPA uses today. Barrel aging the beer for a year mitigated the hops profile substantially. Or such was the presumption, as no one had had the good fortune, and brewery backing and expertise needed, to try it. "Mike was the first gullible idiot who took me up on it ... it's a completely unsustainable project financially" (*as told to Martyn Cornell on the British beer blog Zythophile, September 26, 2016*).

After several months perfecting the recipe with Ron, Goose Island brewers hit on the right historical ingredients (itself an involved process) and recipe. In June 2015, the beer was transferred to bourbon barrels to age for a year with *Brettanomyces clauseneii* yeast, the same variety of wild yeast that a Denmark laboratory found present in a sample of an English stock ale dating to 1903. (British breweries in the nineteenth century would have relied on wild airborne yeast, which gave stock ales their unique flavor.) Over time, the hops mellowed and the beer developed an incredible complexity, with a sour tang and bitter balance. The result, released in very limited quantities in 2016, was one of the most unique beers that we've ever tasted.

THE FLAVORS

TASTING, STORING & SERVING BEER

Curiosity and experimentation lead to discovery and progress.

We are fortunate to live in the most exciting time in beer history. From the cleanest expression of a summery kölsch to a big, funky barrel-aged sour ale, beer today is breaking creative boundaries—arguably more than any other beverage.

In this section, we start with a refresher on the basics of the beer tasting experience followed by the flavor profiles of various beer styles. Afterwards, it's time for a little food pairing fun, from back-pocket basics to some of our favorite outside-the-box pairings. With so many styles of beer and possible food pairings, we can only scratch the surface. That's where you take over. Feel like making gravlax or lamb korma this week? We've included some of our favorite recipes, too. Now we're hungry.

Flavor & Aroma
primary*

+

Mouthfeel & Finish
secondary

=

OVERALL IMPRESSION

*Appearance is also a part of the evaluation process, though this can result in a false perception or bias rather than an accurate understanding of a beer.

THE TASTING EXPERIENCE

There is so much more at work in the tasting experience than what our taste buds tell us. Beyond the flavor, the appearance, aromas, mouthfeel, and finish of a food or drink are equal players. How the flavors of a certain beer change the flavors of a given food can create a completely new flavor experience.

APPEARANCE: Color, Carbonation & Clarity

The appearance of a beer, more than any other quality, has the power to influence our expectations about what that beer will taste like. Do you shy away from stouts because they look "too heavy"? Or maybe an unfiltered beer doesn't look as "clean" as you are used to seeing in a beer. What about how it smells? Before we smell or taste the beer in front of us, we typically judge anything we may eat or drink based on its appearance.

The word appearance in beer-speak typically refers to the visual carbonation (does the beer have a lot of bubbles?), the head formation (is the foam thick?), and the overall color and clarity of a beer (is the beer actually light in color, or just very clear rather than cloudy?).

COLOR VERSUS Clarity

Clarity is a part of the filtration process, but the types of malts used in brewing can contribute to the cloudiness or haziness of a beer. Wheat, for instance, can make one beer appear cloudier than others.

LIL' SMOKEY

Malts that have been smoked are an exception to the color-over-flavor rule. Smoking gives malts distinct flavors like mesquite, hickory, and peat. To balance their intensity, smoked malts are typically blended with malts that have not been smoked. Brewers can also give a beer these flavors by adding smoky ingredients like lapsang souchong tea during or after the brewing process.

Color

A beer can be as light as wheat bread, like the lightest lagers, or as dark as black coffee, like some porters and stouts. A beer's color largely depends on how much the malt or combination of malts was roasted before brewing.

Other Color Determinants Nothing is ever as simple as it seems, right? Beyond how much the malted grains are toasted, adjunct or "added" ingredients and whether/how a beer was aged also play a role in a beer's final color.

Lolita is a Belgian-style pale ale variation that uses a fairly standard malt bill as far as beer color is concerned (primarily 2-row and caramel malts). After the brewing process, Lolita is aged in wine barrels with ripe raspberries, which contributes to the beer's rosy color.

Standard Reference Method (SRM)

The SRM is a rating system developed by the American Society of Brewing Chemists (ASBC) and used by both professional and home brewers. It categorizes the color of a beer by specifying the finished beer color based on the malt bill (or combination of malts) used for brewing. The color rating of the actual malt grain is determined by the color that a single type of malt turns the wort during the boiling process. Technically, the SRM value is 12.7 times the log of the attenuation experienced by light of wavelength 430 nanometers in passing through 1 cm of the wort. (What the? Right.) The scaling factor of 12.7 was chosen to correspond to values measured in the previous industry rating system, known as Lovibond, which dates to the 1860s. The two terms, SRM and Lovibond, are often used interchangeably by both professional and home brewers.

The rating system ranges from 1, a very pale, straw-like color, to 40+, a value that beer professionals typically describe as very dark brown or black. For perspective, 312 Urban Wheat Ale has an SRM of around 4.5, while Winter Ale hits at what most consider the higher end of the SRM scale at 45 (a rich, dark brown color). More recent style additions to the beer world push that color spectrum to its limits. Our 2016 Bourbon County Brand Stout, for example, clocks in at 170 SRM, and the 2016 Rare Bourbon County Brand Stout has a massive 260 SRM—even our brewers aren't sure what to call that color.

Carbonation

Carbonation, in terms of appearance, is both the head on top of a beer (technically, the carbon dioxide being released from that beer) and the bubbly effervescence within the beer (the carbon dioxide dissolved in the liquid). Carbonation is also important to how you smell a beer, as the bubbles release aromatics into the air as they rise to the surface. It also influences mouthfeel (see page 169).

Examining the carbonation can reveal several clues about the beer:
• Less carbonation, as in cask ales, can lead to a "flatter" mouthfeel.
• Smaller bubbles, like those in nitrogenated beers, can result in a "creamy" mouthfeel.

A big, foamy head and a lot of bubbles can lead to a "prickly" mouthfeel. This gives the perception of lightening the weightiness in the beer by mitigating any viscosity and/or lingering flavors of that beer.

Clarity

With wine, those with greater clarity are often thought to be of higher quality. With beer, clarity has no bearing on quality; the clarity of a beer, from crystal clear to very cloudy or hazy, only offers hints about the ingredients used, the style of that beer, and/or how a beer was likely finished.

Clear A clear or "clean-looking" beer is one that has been filtered to physically or chemically remove the yeast from the beer. Noticing the clarity before you take a sip will give clues as to the type of beer. Beers that are meant to be crisp and refreshing, like a pilsner or kölsch, are typically filtered.

Cloudy or Hazy A beer that is cloudy in appearance is typically "unfiltered," a term that refers to the yeast being left in the beer. Sometimes, a large amount of grains, especially wheat and oats, were also used in the brewing process. Belgian-style Witbier is a traditional example where both the yeast and the high level of grain cause the cloudy appearance. Cloudiness in beers is often a hint that the beer will likely have a fuller mouthfeel and more complex flavors and aromas.

Exceptions: While a hazy appearance could also mean a beer has soured or spoiled unintentionally, more often than not, it is simply a reflection of the intended style.

OTHER "HAZE" CAUSES

Beyond unfiltered or grain-rich beers, there are other reasons a beer may appear hazy. Some are indicative of the style, while others are not desirable qualities.

Hop Haze As with any plant, the vegetative matter in hops can combine with protein compounds, found in malt, to cause a haze. That haze could indicate an unwanted bitterness and astringency, or just as likely, it is due to another factor and does not adversely affect the flavors or aromas—and can actually add to them.

Chill Haze Beer that is stored at temperatures that are too cold will develop a haziness when the proteins from the malts bond with the polyphenols from the hops. When the beer warms up, the haze typically dissipates.

Bartender Haze If a retail establishment doesn't clean its tap lines well, it can result in cloudy and off-tasting beer.

Beer Color—SRM Guide

Use this chart as a general guideline, while keeping in mind that there will always be overlap in styles that exhibit ranges above or below those stated here, and those that appear in various categories. Individual batches of a beer will also vary in color. Green Line, for instance, averages 7 SRM but can range from 5 to 9 SRM.

STANDARD REFERENCE METHOD

DEGREE ROASTED	BEER COLOR	STYLES OF BEER	GOOSE BEERS
Light SRM 1 to 5	Shortbread cookies, raw oats, latte	German, Czech & American-style pilsners, Kölsch, blonde ales	312 Urban Wheat Ale, Summertime Kölsch, Sofie, Halia*
Medium-Light SRM 5 to 10	Untoasted walnuts, cedar, wheat bread	English country ales, IPAs	Goose IPA, Four Star Pils, Green Line, Gillian*
Medium SRM 10-15	Lightly toasted walnuts, wheat bread	English bitters, IPAs, double IPAs, Belgian Pale Ales	Honkers Ale, The Illinois, Matilda, Juliet*
Medium-Dark SRM 15 to 20	Darkly toasted walnuts, wheat bread, cappuccino	Amber ales	2016 Fall Experimental, Lolita*
Dark SRM 20 to 30	Coffee with a splash of cream	Amber & nut-brown ales	Goose Oktoberfest, Madame Rose*
Very Dark SRM 30 to 50	Flourless chocolate cake	Winter warmers, porters, many stouts	Winter Ale, Christmas dAle
Darkest SRM 50+	Black coffee or espresso	Aged stouts & barleywines	Bourbon County Brand Stout series

*The SRM of the Sour Sisters is largely influenced by the color of the fruit addition. Halia (white peaches) is lower on the scale, while Madame Rose (cherries) is the darkest at around 22 SRM.

Bottle Conditioning Because of the yeast, an unfiltered beer will continue to develop complex flavors and aromatics in the form of "esters" from the yeast, a process known as bottle-conditioning. In England, unfiltered draft releases are known as cask-conditioned beers, or "real ale."

All of our barrel-aged beers are unfiltered, including the Sour Sisters, Sofie, and the Bourbon County Brand Stout series. Matilda, 312 Urban Wheat Ale, and many of the experimental beers in the Fulton & Wood series and other series are also unfiltered.

CASK-CONDITIONED or "REAL ALE"

In England, cask-conditioned ales made in accordance with strict guidelines are called "real ales." The beer must be made with traditional ingredients, matured or "conditioned" in an eleven-gallon cask to undergo secondary fermentation, and then served from the same cask. The name was developed by CAMRA, or the Campaign for Real Ale, an independent group of beer enthusiasts who banded together in 1973 to protect the authenticity and quality of English ale. At the time, very carbonated, pasteurized beers had become the main pub offering. This trend would soon be mimicked in the United States, where light lagers would eventually dominate our beer market—the catalyst for a humble Chicago beer enthusiast across the pond to produce his own quality ales. We always have a cask beer on draft at the Fulton Street Taproom. For more on the early history of Goose Island, see page 11.

FLAVOR

The six basic components of taste detected by our tongues are **bitter**, **sour**, **salty**, **fatty**, **sweet**, and the #hashtag of the taste bud world, **umami**.

Beyond these six common flavors, everyone's taste receptors and impressions are different and, in an ideal tasting world, always evolving.

Flavor Commonalities

Some flavor components are easy to detect. Some bags of popcorn are so salted that "salty" is the universal way to describe their taste. Sweetness from one-dimensional sources like sugar is also easy to separate from other flavors.

These flavor commonalities, flavors that we as a society recognize and agree upon, set the standards for describing categories of foods and beverages. Other flavors, like umami, are trickier to nail down to a single flavor sensation.

Perception versus Reality

We all know someone who swears he or she doesn't like something before even trying it. Those biases aren't limited to weekend brunches. Even professional wine and beer critics can have a hard time leaving their prejudices at the door, which is why most professional tastings are blind.

How we perceive flavor certainly depends on our experiences. How can one describe the flavor of fennel if they've never tasted it? One person's fennel may just be another person's licorice.

"IN 1995, WE ENTERED THE FIRST BOURBON COUNTY STOUT

in the Great American Beer Festival in the Russian Imperial Stout category. It was the only option. We got disqualified for the beer's 'odd flavors.' It was too smoky to one judge, too sweet to another. It didn't fit the expected example of what a Russian Imperial Stout 'should' be. And then we had other people come up to us saying that it was the best beer in the competition, that it should win a gold medal in something, and 'Who cares which category?' People used words to describe it like licorice and even coconut. Words that people weren't used to using for any beer back then, they were using to describe Bourbon County Stout."

—Greg Hall, Goose Island brewmaster 1991–2011
Founder, Virtue Cider Company, Greater Chicago Area

A new style category, Wood and Barrel-Aged Strong Stout, was added at the Great American Beer Festival after the introduction of **Bourbon County Stout.**

AROMA

A hound dog may beat us to the truffles, but the human olfactory system is remarkably advanced. Smell makes up more than three-quarters of what we know as "flavor." There are thousands of smells that affect our sensory perception.

Try this age-old trick: close your nose before tasting something, then taste the same thing again *after* inhaling. Welcome to a whole new flavor world.

Aroma Building Blocks

The olfactory system can detect thousands of smells. Each of those smells are different chemical compounds. Some are detectable when you breathe in, others when you breathe out. Throughout a lifetime, the sensory system constantly takes in new aromas that are registered and categorized by your olfactory system. All the more reason to keep smelling—and tasting—new things.

Sense Memory

Smell, more so than any other sense, evokes the most emotion. We all have smells that make us recall certain memories—mixing a batch of lemonade for a sidewalk stand, baking holiday cookies with the family. It's no coincidence that the olfactory system is located in the limbic system, the same place the brain registers memory, emotion, and behavior.

Consider choosing a beer that evokes aroma memories. Crisp beers with aromatics of freshly cut grass and summer fruits, like 312 Urban Wheat Ale or Summertime Kölsch, are natural fits for summer gatherings. Winter Ale, a malty, balanced beer with toasted spice and caramel aromas, gets the nostalgia going at holiday parties.

PIONEERING PINT

The flavor of an India Pale Ale is often described as "hoppy and dry" because those qualities are often representative of the style. Does that mean all IPAs have those qualities? To some extent, yes, but like most things in the beer world, not necessarily. Today more than ever, the best brewers are exploring the whole of their creative space, pushing beyond traditional flavor boundaries into uncharted territory while at the same time digging deep into history to find lost interpretations of known styles. This is one of the many reasons brewing is so exciting right now.

A basic understanding of the typical qualities in any given beer style acts as a reference point for getting to that uncharted flavor place. At Goose Island, we embrace experimentation so fully, we've created a physical space at the brewery to serve as an incubator for creativity among our brewers (see Pilot Brewery, page 46).

Aroma Perception and Variance

There is no right or wrong way to describe a beer's aromas. Each of us has different aroma experiences, something that a complex beverage like beer fully embraces. Your opinion is as valuable as the brewer's notes.

Rasselbock

The name **Rasselbock** from our Fulton & Wood series (see page 145) is a reference to the rasselbock, an imaginary rabbit creature with wings from German folklore. In a nod to that mythology, the brewing team combined the qualities of a doppelbock, roggenbier, and Bavarian weiss to create a dark ale brewed with Weihenstephan yeast, a traditional German strain, and a blend of rye and wheat malts.

Brewer / Bottle Aroma Description Banana and clove aromatics
Fan Aroma Descriptions
Most Common Clove, warm spices, banana, rye, yeast
Other Toasted bread, soft pretzel, caramel, toffee, nuts, pink peppercorns, leather, grass, bubblegum, dark fruit, raspberry, orange peel, apple

Matilda

According to legend, a grateful Countess Mathilda founded a monastery where, over centuries, monks have been brewing ale that is unique in character. While in Belgium, we were inspired by the story and the great Trappist ales. We returned to Chicago and brewed our homage with the wild yeast *Brettanomyces,* and a Belgian-style pale ale named Matilda was born.

Brewer / Bottle Aroma Description Dried fruit and clove aromatics
Fan Aroma Descriptions
Most Common Dried apricot, mandarin, orange, citrus, clove, cinnamon biscuit
Other Orange marmalade, banana, peach, sour white grapes, spring lilies, anise, honey, oatmeal cookies, blondie cookie bars

The Illinois Imperial IPA

The first Imperial beer of the year, the Illinois is an homage to the mile-high skyscraper Frank Lloyd Wright designed for the city of Chicago that was never built. Had it been, Chicago's skyscraper would still be the tallest building in the world today. This IPA is equally towering, pushing the limits of hop flavor and aroma.

Brewer / Bottle Aroma Description Complex citrus and hops aromatics
Fan Aroma Descriptions
Most Common Citrus, orange, hops, pine
Other Lemon, grapefruit, earthy, herbal, peppery

MOUTHFEEL

Mouthfeel is literally the sense of touch in your mouth. Does a beer feel light-bodied as you sip, like skim milk, or does it feel weightier and more full-bodied, almost coating your tongue, like heavy cream? Maybe it is somewhere in between, in the 2% milk range? Does the beer feel prickly from the effervescence, like a highly carbonated pilsner, or the opposite, as with a smooth, nitrogenated stout? Do you feel heat in both your chest and in the exhaust as you breathe out after a sip? These qualities are known as mouthfeel and are a combination of physical and chemical sensations.

In beverages, mouthfeel may be barely detectable or a dominant quality in the overall tasting experience. This quality is often overlooked, yet mouthfeel is incredibly important in determining the true experience of the beer. Mouthfeel lends a depth of character to the often more pronounced senses of aroma and taste.

Mouthfeel Qualities in Beer Common descriptions of mouthfeel in beer include light, refreshing, crisp, prickly, chalky, dry, coarse, sharp, creamy, oily, thick, warming, heavy, viscous, syrupy, chewy, warm or hot, and so on.

Finish ... AKA Aftertaste

The aromas, flavors, and mouthfeel that remain after taking a bite or a sip can be very subtle and disappear quickly, or, they may be more dominant and make a lasting impression. The best way to experience aftertaste is to line up different styles and intensities of beer, from lightest to the most intense. A crisp, refreshing beer might have a few detectable citrusy aromas and subtle lingering flavors. Take a sip of an intensely flavored brew like any beer in the Bourbon County Brand Stout series, and you can expect a bold aftertaste and lingering finish.

The word *aftertaste* has a bad reputation, which is why we prefer to use the word *finish*. Many people who claim to be non-beer drinkers frequently say that beer has a "bad aftertaste." The finish of beer can be bitter and strong in a good way, like coffee or dark chocolate. Beer is as diverse as food. Not all beers should have a brief, crisp, clean finish. While that is great in a beer like 312 Urban Wheat Ale, a similar finish wouldn't be appropriate in a fruity, sour ale like barrel-aged Lolita, a complex beer that lingers and changes on the palate like fine wine.

MAKING A DRY Impression

The word "tannic" is typically used to describe wine with a dry mouthfeel, a quality derived from the skin of grapes. With beer, the sensation of a dry finish is especially detectable in hop-forward beers like Goose IPA. In the beverage industry, a truly "dry" drink must lack sugar. Beer is not truly dry, as it contains sugar from malt and other ingredients, but hops still get us to the same place.

Changing Beer Perceptions

Wine is often considered an "easy sell" at high-end restaurants. When developing an equally respected beer program, educating customers by offering parallels between the overall qualities beer and wine styles have in common can be the catalyst for opening minds to new experiences.

Sofie
Brewer Description Sparkling with dry finish
Wine Parallel Dry with notes of white pepper like Brut Champagne or Grüner Veltliner

Matilda
Brewer Description Earthy, medium bodied
Wine Parallel Red Burgundy or a similar balanced red wine

Goose IPA
Brewer Description Bold citrus aromatics, crisp finish
Wine Parallel Dry, acidic white like Albariño

Four Star Pils
Brewer Description Dry, refreshing
Wine Parallel Dry and herbaceous German whites like Riesling or Silvaner

Madame Rose
Brewer Description Tart, dry, and complex
Wine Parallel Medium-bodied acidic reds like Bordeaux or Nebbiolo

Bourbon County Brand Stout
Brewer Description Bold, rich, complex
Wine Parallel Port, Banyuls, or a similar intense, rich dessert wine

Setting up a Beer Tasting

Evaluating beer is a formal process with industry-wide parameters. That doesn't mean a tasting experience has to involve dozens of beers, or that a more casual tasting can't be equally as informative.

With fewer beers to experience, tasters gain a deeper understanding of each style, whether at an event or one-on-one in a retail establishment. As tasters move through the beers, have them give a brief explanation of the style and basic characteristics of each. And by all means, have a little fun. "Formal" doesn't have to be boring.

Lightest to Heaviest Kick off with a big, barrel-aged stout, and your palate is going to be in overdrive from the start. Taste beers with lighter, more nuanced flavors first before moving on to bolder brews.

Alcohol Content Generally, beers with a high alcohol content are going to have a "stronger" effect on the palate than lower-alcohol beers. They also tend to be on the "heavier" end of the flavor spectrum. Bring out those higher ABV beers, like Bourbon County Brand Stout, toward the end of a tasting.

Tasting Beer like a Brewer

How does a brewer taste beer while on the clock? Methodically, and with a tasting log in hand to take notes. Off the clock, anything goes. As one of our brewers likes to say, "If it's good, drink it." Word.

Pour and examine the beer
Look at the color, clarity, carbonation.

Gently swirl, then inhale
Swirling helps release the aromatics. Are they subtle or more pronounced? What scents are you picking up?

Slowly sip
Not too much, or the liquid will speed past your palate. What are the basic flavors? Are you detecting certain ingredients? Are some more subtle than others? How is the mouthfeel? Sip cautiously, or consider using a dump bucket if there are more beers to taste.

Consider the aftertaste and aromas
Is there a lingering aftertaste, a certain flavor? Or is the aftertaste more generally dry or sweet? Aromas? What is your overall impression of the beer?

Cleanse the palate
If you are tasting multiple beers, take a sip of water before moving on to the next sample.

Finished?
Great. Now, enjoy the hops out of that beer.

"ONE OF THE GREAT THINGS ABOUT TASTING

straight, classic Bourbon County is that you can go through a glass, and each sip is telling a little bit different story. You're getting coffee, you're getting vanilla, and then you're getting coconut. It's always something new."

—Greg Hall, Goose Island brewmaster 1991–2011
Founder, Virtue Cider Company, Greater Chicago Area

Tasting Tools

If you're hosting a more formal tasting, both a Tasting Wheel and Tasting Record will be helpful to have on hand for participants. The Tasting Wheel serves as a visual reminder of the incredible complexity in the aroma, flavor, mouthfeel, aftertaste, and even clarity of different beers. Each taster can come to his or her own conclusions on his or her Tasting Record.

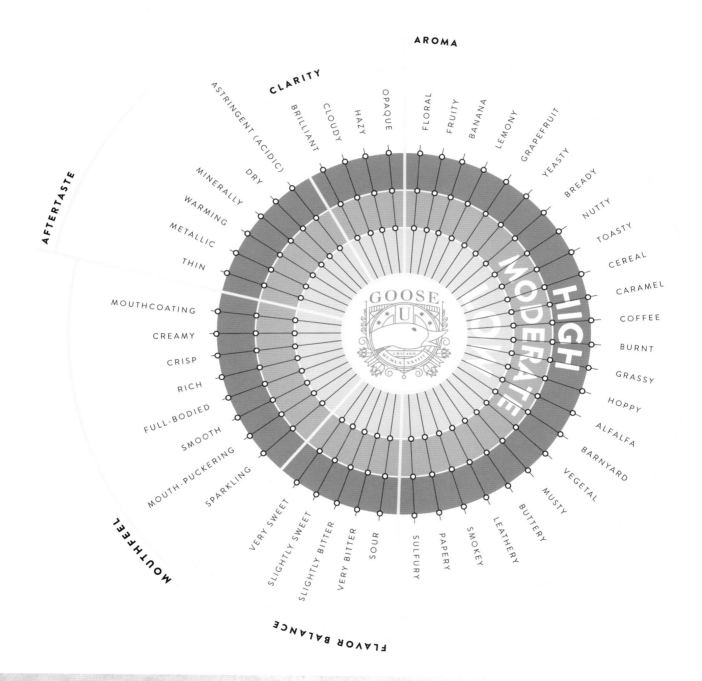

TASTING RECORD

DATE

LOCATION

BEER

ABV

TYPE / STYLE

IBU

APPREARANCE: _____

     COLOR: _____

     CLARITY: _____

AROMA: _____
_____
_____

FLAVOR BALANCE: _____
_____
_____

MOUTHFEEL: _____
_____
_____

AFTERTASTE: _____
_____

OVERALL IMPRESSION: _____
_____
_____

SPECIFIC OFF-FLAVORS AND AROMAS:

- ○ ACIDIC (VINEGAR)
- ○ ALCOHOLIC
- ○ ASTRINGENT / HARSH
- ○ EARTHY / CORKED
- ○ CHEESY

- ○ CHLOROPHENOL (BANDAGE)
- ○ DIACETYL (BUTTERY)
- ○ DMS (CREAMED CORN)
- ○ ESTERY / SOLVENTY
- ○ METALLIC

- ○ OXIDIZED
- ○ SKUNKED
- ○ SULFURIC / SULFIDIC
- ○ OTHER: _____

TEMPERATURE

Beer has been enjoyed for thousands of years, long before the invention of temperature-controlled beverage refrigerators. In places like Britain, beer was stored below ground in a cellar or a similar space where temperatures were naturally cooler and climate-controlled. The flavor nuances in certain styles—like a British-style ale, ESB (Extra-Special Bitter), or stout—really come through at those slightly warmer cellar serving temperatures.

STORING & SERVING BEER

When the brewing and aging process is complete, the hard work of preserving the quality of our beer begins

In a restaurant or bar setting, especially in the era of instant social media reviews, maintaining quality is fundamental to the retail establishment. When developing a top-quality retail beer program, keep the following storage and service factors in mind: **storage temperature**, **age**, **serving temperature**, and **glassware**.

Stale Beer

With some beverages, the signs of spoilage are obvious. Milk takes on a pungent sour smell and buttermilk-like flavors, while wine takes on distinct musty, vinegary, and/or cooked fruit qualities.

When beer begins to stale, the aroma, flavor, clarity, and body (mouthfeel) can be affected in subtler ways. The beer will develop unique off notes, maybe subtly cardboard-like or leathery aromas, tart and sour flavors like green apple, or sweet honey or butterscotch notes—again, depending on the beer style. Those same qualities can be *desirable* characteristics in other beer styles, which can make the detection of off notes difficult for untrained staff.

SKUNKED BEER

Light damage occurs when hops or hop extracts are exposed to ultraviolet light sources, which can cause what is known as a "skunked" flavor in beer. Green and clear bottles offer little to no protection. The most protective color is brown, a discovery that made amber-hued bottles popular again in the early twentieth century (amber bottles in the "export style" had been used at least since the mid-1800s on cargo ships for beer, cider, soda, and other beverages). Goose Island beer is packaged in amber-colored bottles or, more recently, aluminum cans, which also offer protection from light damage.

Regardless of the packaging, beer should never be stored in an area with bright light, including storerooms with fluorescent lighting, as light damage can still occur.

Storage Temperature

Beer doesn't belong in a hot storage room any more than wine does. Protect your investment with a good-quality storage system.

Today, most lagers and lighter ales are typically stored in the refrigerator at around 35°F. Sour and other wild yeast-fermented ales and richer porters and stouts (including barrel-aged beers) should be stored at or near cellar temperature, around 55°F.

Heat Effects Beer stored at temperatures that are too warm can result in oxidation, causing metallic, "wet cardboard," or other off flavors to develop. Storing beer at warmer temperatures also shortens its shelf life.

In a widely cited beer industry study known as the **3-30-300 rule**, virtually the same flavor loss results in beer stored for three days in ninety-degree heat (the average summer day) as in beer stored for thirty days at room temperature (approximately 72°F). Because carbon dioxide expands as it heats, the beer will also lose carbonation. A beer stored at very cold temperatures (around 33°F, colder than a refrigerator) can be stored for up to 300 days. The chilled beer will also retain more carbon dioxide.

Freezing Point At the opposite end, freezing beer causes the alcohol in the beer to separate. The thawed beer will have a cloudy appearance and will also suffer from carbonation damage.

The freezing temperature of beer varies depending on the alcohol content and style. This is especially important to keep in mind with many aged beers, as higher-alcohol beers freeze at lower temperatures.

SERVICE TIP

Multi-purpose snifters can be used to enjoy a Bourbon County Brand Stout one night and the next, a classic brandy or cognac—or bourbon aged in the same barrels as the stout.

AGE

Always ask a beer its age. Some, like IPAs, are best served "young" (typically within six months) to preserve the more delicate aroma and flavor qualities. Others, like wild fermented sour ales or barrel-aged stouts, can be cellared for months or even years to allow the complexity to develop further.

Check the label for the maximum shelf life or aging potential of each Goose Island beer. Many of our beers are brewed to be enjoyed within 180 days of bottling. The Sour Sisters, beers in the Bourbon County Stout series, and other aged beers can be enjoyed right away, or allowed to develop in the bottle for up to five years.

LESS THAN 180 DAYS 312 Urban Wheat Ale, Goose IPA, Four Star Pils, Honkers Ale, Green Line, The Illinois, Summertime Kölsch, Fest Bier, Winter Ale, and many limited-release ales and lagers

UP TO FIVE YEARS Sofie, Matilda, the Sour Sisters (Halia, Gillian, Lolita, Juliet, Madame Rose), Bourbon County Brand Stout (Original, Coffee, Proprietor's, Barleywine, and special releases), and other wild yeast or barrel-aged beers

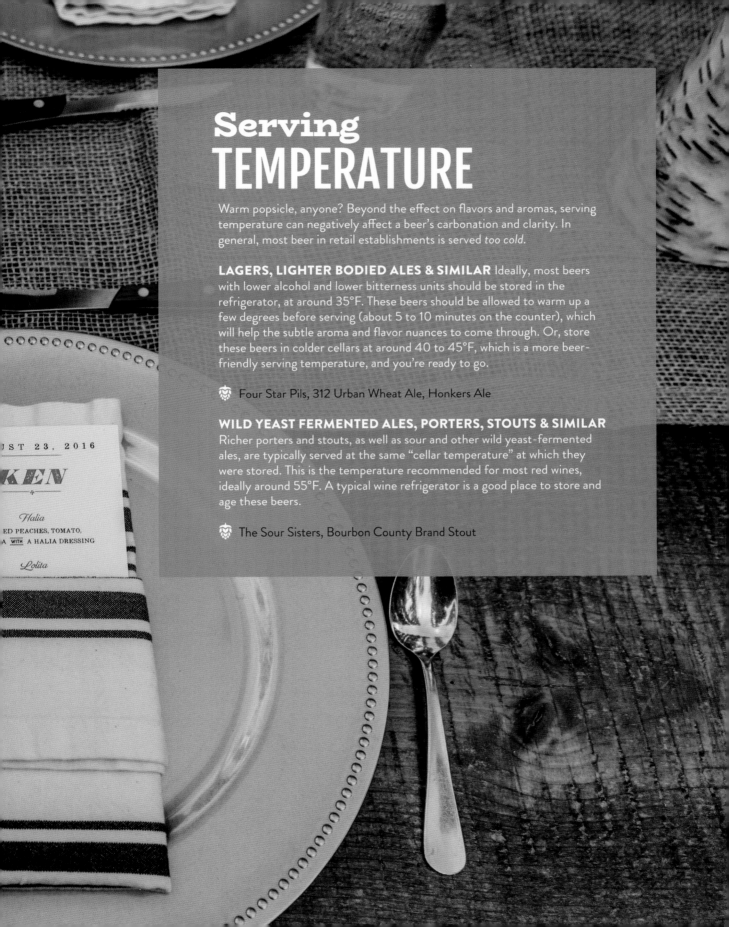

Serving
TEMPERATURE

Warm popsicle, anyone? Beyond the effect on flavors and aromas, serving temperature can negatively affect a beer's carbonation and clarity. In general, most beer in retail establishments is served *too cold*.

LAGERS, LIGHTER BODIED ALES & SIMILAR Ideally, most beers with lower alcohol and lower bitterness units should be stored in the refrigerator, at around 35°F. These beers should be allowed to warm up a few degrees before serving (about 5 to 10 minutes on the counter), which will help the subtle aroma and flavor nuances to come through. Or, store these beers in colder cellars at around 40 to 45°F, which is a more beer-friendly serving temperature, and you're ready to go.

Four Star Pils, 312 Urban Wheat Ale, Honkers Ale

WILD YEAST FERMENTED ALES, PORTERS, STOUTS & SIMILAR Richer porters and stouts, as well as sour and other wild yeast-fermented ales, are typically served at the same "cellar temperature" at which they were stored. This is the temperature recommended for most red wines, ideally around 55°F. A typical wine refrigerator is a good place to store and age these beers.

The Sour Sisters, Bourbon County Brand Stout

GLASSWARE

Would you ideally serve Champagne in a red wine glass? As with sparkling wine, smelling a beer's incredible aromas through the peephole opening of a bottle or can is difficult. Even still, whenever possible, a glass is always the best choice. With more space to open up, the beer's aromas and flavors will be more detectable. Using appropriate glassware also helps keep the beer's temperature more stable and maintains the proper head (foam) for the style.

CLEANLINESS Leftover dish soap, musty cabinets, lingering food smells … nothing spoils beer more quickly than a glass that isn't as clean as it looks. **A dirty glass is the number-one culprit in an "off" beer or wine tasting at a restaurant or other retail establishment.**

IS IT A "BEER-CLEAN" GLASS?

Lacing Test After each sip, the beer's foam should evenly adhere to the inside of the glass in parallel rings. If the foam does not make parallel rings, a quality known as **lacing**, the glass is likely dirty.

Sheeting (Water) Test Dunk a glass in water. A clean glass will be evenly coated in a "sheet" of water. Bubbles or droplets clinging to the side of the glass indicate the water—or worse, the beer, if the drink has already been poured—is clinging to some contaminant. Soap and food residues are the usual suspects. Yum.

Salt Test Wet the inside of the glass and shake out the excess water. Sprinkle plenty of iodized salt evenly throughout the glass and give it a nice swirl to coat. If the glass is clean, the salt will evenly adhere to the inside of the glass. If dirty, the salt will not evenly adhere to the glass. Grease and other contaminants will cause the salt to adhere in an uneven pattern.

BEER GLASSWARE

CHALICE	NONIC PINT	SNIFTER	PILSNER	WEIZEN

Glassware Shapes Most good-quality restaurants and other retail establishments keep three core wine glasses on hand: red and white glasses and a Champagne flute. As with wine, stocking the proper glassware for different styles of beer doesn't require investing in every glass shape available. Goose Island's beers are served and enjoyed at their optimal profiles in the following glassware.

GLASSWARE

The brewery produces logo glassware in several shapes. Check with your local wholesaler for availability.

Goose Vintage Glassware, Chalice
Goose Pint Glass, Nonic
Goose Imperial Stout Glass, Snifter
Goose Pilsner Glass, Pilsner
Goose Stange, the traditional Kölsch glass for summer
Goose Stein, Fest Bier

SHAKING THE SHAKER

The shaker pint, an American draft beer standard since the 1980s, couldn't be more appropriately named. The glass was originally used with a metal cup as a cocktail shaker to mix drinks—not to drink them. With its uniform shape, the American pint glass allows subtle beer aromas and carbon dioxide to quickly escape, causing the head to dissipate. The workhorse nature of the thick, sturdy glass hasn't helped beer lovers, either. Beyond mixing cocktails, shaker pints are often used to serve everything from ice water to soda. When glassware hits the dishwasher more frequently, the chance of a soapy-residue tasting disaster is not far behind.

Core Beer Glassware

Keep these five core glass shapes on hand, and you're ready to serve any beer.

Chalice or Goose Vintage Glassware

Shape Stemmed, medium-small bowl with concave taper, outward flared rim; resembles namesake flower term

Benefits Warm hands do not touch glass; taper holds aroma; flare encourages foamy head

Example Styles Belgian Ales (pale to strong), Double IPAs, Lambics, Farmhouse Ales, Bière de Garde, Specialty Beers (herb and other rich aromas)

 Sofie, Matilda, Sour Sisters: Gillian, Halia, Juliet, Lolita, Madame Rose

Nonic ("No-Nick") Pint or Goose Pint Glass

Shape Stemless, cylindrical, "bump" near top, medium-wide mouth (narrower than American Shaker pint)

Benefits Height encourages foamy head; bump makes glass easy to hold/prevents chipping/limits warm hand exposure; narrower mouth encourages foam retention

Example Styles Amber Ales, American Lager, Brown Ales, English Bitters, Irish Red, Pale Ales (IPA, Pilsner), Porter, Stout

 Goose IPA, 312 Urban Wheat Ale, Four Star Pils, Green Line, Honkers Ale, The Illinois, Summertime Kölsch, Autumn Ale, C.A.L.M. Radler, Festivity Ale, Fest Bier,* Summer Ale, Fulton & Wood Rasselbock

*The stein is the traditional glass for Fest Bier. The style dates to the early 1800s and was used for beers served outdoors. The early lidded versions were crafted out of copper, ceramics, or other sturdy materials. Today most, like the Goose Stein, are made of glass and no longer have a lid.

Snifter

Shape Stemmed, goblet-like with wide bowl, inward curved rim

Benefits Hands can warm glass; plenty of swirling room; narrow at the top for carbonation retention and maximum aromatic experience.

Example Styles Barleywine, Strong Ales, Quadrupels, Barrel-Aged Beers, Russian Imperial Stout

 Bourbon County Brand Stout series: Classic, Coffee, Proprietor's, Rare, Rye, Regal Rye, Barleywine

Pilsner Glass

Shape Stemless, tall, and slender, slightly wider rim

Benefits Slender design to release carbonation; wider top retains foam and releases aromas

Example Styles American Lagers, Pilsners

 Four Star Pils, Preseason Lager, and other limited-release beers including Natural Villain

Weizen (Weissbier) Glass

Shape Stemless, tall, and slender; narrow base with distinctive upper bell-shaped curve, inward curved rim (often confused with a Pilsner glass)

Benefits Slender design to release carbonation; curve near top traps and encourages thick head and locks in banana and clove-like phenols

Example Styles German and American Wheat Beers

 312 Urban Wheat Ale, Summertime Kölsch,* C.A.L.M. Radler, Fulton & Wood Rasselbock, and other limited-release beers

*The traditional glass for serving Kölsch is a stange (German for stick or rod), and it has a tall, narrow shape and thin glass walls. Though a Nonic pint or better still, a tall Weizen glass works well, the Goose Stange is perfect for enjoying the light, refreshing beer style (see page 98).

BEER & FOOD PAIRING

At Goose Island, we believe every rule is meant to be broken.

Becoming a rule breaker first requires the knowledge and experience to make informed decisions. This section offers an overview of beer styles and food pairing suggestions to get you started.

Keep in mind that what follows is a brief foundation, a jumping-off point from which to start your race. There is so much more to explore beneath the surface of these pages on your own. Digest, ruminate, talk to brewers and beer experts, read other sources, and by all means, eat, drink, and repeat. We all benefit from becoming experts at the craft of enjoying beer and food together, and then coming up with our own combinations.

BEER & FOOD PAIRING BASICS

Start with basic metrics by finding parallel and contrasting traits. Beer relies on its carbonation, bitterness, and tannic astringency to clean the palate. For instance, a beer brewed with wheat, like Sofie or 312 Urban Wheat Ale, works nicely for brunch with eggs Benedict because the bubbles clean the palate of the creamy viscosity of the eggs and hollandaise—not to mention because of the complementing citrus flavors. Hop-forward beers like Green Line or Goose IPA, with their bitterness and dryness, can stand up to more intense flavors and creamy sauces (an herbaceous béarnaise, a spicy curry). A big, malty beer like Bourbon County Brand Barleywine or the original Bourbon County Brand Stout pairs nicely with equally big, rich desserts.

Yes, it really can be that easy. Jump right in. What are you waiting for? Some pairings probably won't work, which means you're doing something right. Tweet us @Goose_Island #nailedit and tell us all about it. Failure takes us all to uncharted places.

Find Parallel Traits Looking for common flavor characteristics between any food and beverage is one of the most reliable places to begin thinking about pairings. For example, the bold qualities of an IPA play off equally big flavors like blue cheese, bacon-wrapped dates, a smoky burger, blackened chicken, grilled shrimp, and spicy chili. Bring it on.

Pairing Tip Avoid the temptation to go overboard when relying on common traits for a pairing. A very malty, sweet beer can be overwhelmed by a very sweet dessert. Together, it becomes difficult for the palate to pick up the subtle characteristics in both the beer and food.

Highlight Contrasting Traits Sweet and sour, salty and spicy, bitter and sweet. Opposite flavor pairings are at the core of some of the greatest dishes and cuisines, and even of such everyday spice pairings as salt and pepper. The same principles can be applied to beer and food pairings. A malty beer with a sweet finish like Honkers Ale pairs well with salty pub fare like traditional fish and chips or English cheddar. A hop-forward beer like Goose IPA takes on its sweet opposite in a surprising dessert match: carrot cake.

Pairing Tip When working with contrasting flavors, match strength with strength. A subtly flavored cheese, like Brie, needs an equally nuanced beer, like Sofie. A bold, in-your-face blue cheese is balanced by a beer with a towering hop character, like The Illinois.

BEYOND Ingredients

With some dishes, how an ingredient is cooked can be as important to consider as the ingredients themselves. Grilled shrimp typically pairs well with an equally bold beer, like Goose IPA, thanks to the intensely charred, smoky flavor imparted by the grill. The more delicate flavors in sautéed shrimp are typically a better match for a crisp, refreshing beer like 312 Urban Wheat Ale, Four Star Pils, or Summertime Kölsch.

BEER & FOOD FLAVOR INTERACTIONS

When in doubt, turn to these typically winning pairing rules.

Hop bitterness → Balanced by → Sweetness, umami
Goose IPA **+** Caramelized onions, BBQ sauce

Malty sweetness → Balanced by → Spicy hot, acidic
Bourbon County Brand Stout **+** Chipotle peppers

Sour tanginess → Balanced by → Earthy
Juliet **+** Braised lamb shanks

Beware: bitterness *increases* perceived spiciness.

Challenging
PAIRINGS

When a sommelier is stumped, a Certified Cicerone® (someone with significant beer expertise) can save the day, or the meal. Beer stands in as an excellent solution for these notoriously difficult food and wine pairings.

Artichokes Cynarin, a naturally occurring plant acid in artichokes, causes many alcoholic beverages to register as sweet on the palate—the reason why many wines are tricky pairings. Hop-forward beers perform an excellent balancing act to offset the sweetness.

🍺 The Illinois, Goose IPA, Green Line

Asparagus & Brussels Sprouts The sulfur compounds in asparagus and Brussels sprouts can make many wines taste metallic and harsh. Fat-rich foods, like bacon with Brussels sprouts or French hollandaise with asparagus, mitigate those compounds. Beer is another winning pairing—particularly pilsner, lagers, or Belgian-style tripels or farmhouse ales—because it has enough complementary sulfur compounds and vegetal, grassy hops nuance to balance the flavors.

🍺 Four Star Pils, The Ogden, The Illinois, Sofie

Vinaigrette Dressing Wines paired with vinegar-based salad dressings can be overpowered by the acid. Try slightly sweeter, malt-forward beers to balance a tangy dressing. The carbonation in beer also helps cut the fattiness from the oil as well as from additions like pungent cheeses (goat, American blue).

🍺 Honkers Ale, Fest Bier, Winter Ale, Pere Jacques

> # "IN ONE ESTIMATE
>
> *some 2,000 (and counting) flavor compounds are present in beer, whereas perhaps no more than 1,000 impact the character of wine. For beer, the flavor comes from the diversity of grist components: from hops, from yeast, from water, and, in the case of beers such as Lambic, from other microorganisms. And much more besides— fruits, herbs, spices, chocolate, the list goes on. For wine, we are talking just grapes, yeast, and a few other organisms, plus wood. And well, there are beers aged in wood, too."*
>
> —Charles Bamforth
> *Grape vs. Grain: A Historical, Technological, and Social Comparison of Wine and Beer*
> (Cambridge University Press, 2008)

BALANCED

A beer described as balanced is not overly sweet, bitter, sour, or any other trait. In other words: not extreme. A beer that is balanced is *not* one-dimensional by definition; balanced beers can be incredibly nuanced. The word can apply to any style of beer, from crisp and refreshing wheat beers like 312 Urban Wheat Ale to balanced and malty English-style pub beers like Honkers Ale.

Pairing Tip A balanced beer plays to its strengths when equally balanced food flavors are on the table. Pairings run from the traditional, like a meaty burger and fries with an English-style pub ale, to modern combinations like sushi and a pilsner.

Balanced & Crisp
Classic Burgers and fries, pub fare, brats, Mexican food, grilled chicken and pork

Other Thai and Chinese dishes (spicy and/or sweet), mild seafood (white fish, sushi), green salads, greens (spinach, kale), beans, legumes, and quinoa (salads, soups)

 312 Urban Wheat Ale, Four Star Pils, Green Line Pale Ale), Summertime Kölsch, and select limited releases including C.A.L.M. Radler

Balanced & Malty*
Classic Burgers and fries, pub fare, fish and chips, brats

Other Indian curries, shellfish, bacon, caramelized vegetables, candied nuts, oatmeal cookies

 Honkers Ale and select limited releases

For more dominant malt-forward beers, see the Malty section, page 193.

CHEESE

Buttery, Toasty, Fruity, Floral, Earthy, Grassy, Funky, Yeasty, Sharp, Mellow, Complex, Mild, Strong

It's no coincidence that the words used to describe beer work well to describe cheeses as well. Cheese and beer have been kindred spirits for centuries. They have been made and enjoyed side by side on dining tables at monasteries and country farms throughout Europe for centuries.

The diversity of good-quality artisan cheeses and well-crafted beers available today makes pairing a virtually limitless tasting menu of opportunity. Better still, those who love the barnyard funk or earthy sweetness of a good cheese typically appreciate a well-crafted beer.

Pairing Beer shares more than simply terroir with cheese (beer is made from grain and cheese from the milk of animals that eat grain). Both cheese and beer are **fermented** and **aged**. That process allows each style of cheese and beer to develop incredibly nuanced, and often parallel, flavor characteristics.

Choosing similar qualities in both the beer and cheese, like a lighter, un-aged pilsner with fresh, delicate mozzarella, is typically a safe bet. Or, go the opposite route and try pairing opposite flavors in the beer and cheese to bring out one or more qualities.

CHEESE CULTURE

Fast food cheeseburgers, mac 'n cheese, chips and queso ... much as we love artisanal cheese, America has a hundred-year appreciation for processed cheese. Patented in 1916 by American entrepreneur James Kraft, the shelf stable and famously meltable, mild style traces its roots to centuries-old fondue. The secret ingredient in the traditional Swiss hot cheese dip? Wine ... or yes, beer.

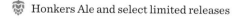

Goose IPA English cheddar
"If it grows together, it goes together," or so the saying goes. Try Goose IPA (an English-style IPA) with an earthy, English-style clothbound cheese like Cabot Clothbound Cheddar aged at Jasper Hill Cellars. While the flavors of the best examples vary throughout the year, this cheese style typically exhibits buttered popcorn and biscuity notes—perfect with a crisp IPA with some of those same toasty flavor parallels and enough tannins to contrast with the buttery cheese.

Goose Honkers Ale Sheep's milk alpine
Ossau-Iraty is a mild, subtle French sheep's milk cheese that is a lovely match for Honkers Ale. Our English-style bitter with quite a bit of maltiness plays well off the toasted wheat and nutty aromas of the cheese.

312 Urban Wheat Ale Fresh chèvre
Bright and refreshing, 312 works incredibly well with a variety of fresh goat cheeses. The cheese shares a bright and tangy quality that mirrors the citrus notes in the beer beautifully. As well as good-quality beer, always choose the best fresh cheese you can find. A good chèvre should be creamy, lemony, and clean-tasting, not chalky; look for those from small, regional producers.

Goose Winter Ale Mild blue
Our Winter Ale is roasty and toasty, with a slightly sweet, malty finish—just the sort of beer for a mild, creamy blue with a nutty backbone. We love Bay Blue from Point Reyes Farmstead Cheese in California or Cashel Blue, an Irish blue cheese.

Goose Summertime Kölsch Burrata
Nothing says summertime like a crisp, refreshing Kölsch. Paired with a fresh, creamy burrata, mozzarella's cool cousin, our German-style ale is the perfect summer entertaining partner and hot-weather pairing.

Goose Island Fest Bier Beaufort-style cheese (Pleasant Ridge Reserve)
The dark, roasty malts in this traditional Märzen-style beer pair well with raw milk Alpine-style cheeses, which are known for their caramelized onion–like sweetness. One of the best American examples is in a class of its own: Pleasant Ridge Reserve, a Beaufort-style cheese from neighboring Wisconsin, is the most awarded cheese in American history.

Sofie Triple crème, bloomy rind
Sofie is a dream come true for lovers of rich cheeses; the effervescent, Champagne-like Saison helps cleanse the palate so you can eat more cheese. For a reminder of Sofie's farmhouse heritage, try a mixed-milk bloomy rind cheese like Zingerman's Manchester from Michigan. Alternatively, pair it with a decadent French triple crème, traditionally paired with Champagne.

Matilda Italian Taleggio
Get funky! Look for a washed-rind cheese that matches Matilda's earthy, funky qualities. Paired together, you get an unforgettable "bacony" sweetness that draws out the subtle fruitiness from the beer. We love a good Italian Taleggio, which, like many great beers, smells much funkier than it tastes.

Halia Aged goat's milk cheese
The bright, sweet peach notes in Halia work incredibly well with the rich, earthy sweetness of an aged goat's milk cheese. Brabander from L'Amuse in Holland is an excellent choice, or look for Midnight Moon from California's Cypress Grove.

Madame Rose Cave-aged blue cheddar
Bold and full of wild yeasts, fruits, and eighteen months of barrel-aging complexity, Madame Rose needs a cheese to match. A cave-aged cheddar like Dunbarton Blue from Roelli Cheese Haus in Wisconsin is mildly inoculated with blue mold to emphasize the earthy and fruity qualities in both the cheese and the beer.

Bourbon County Brand Stout Cheese roulette
Finding a cheese that is big enough to stand up to the inky richness of any of the beers in the Bourbon County Brand Stout series is tricky. Think of these cheeses like desserts: L'Amuse Two-Year Gouda is toffee-like with the texture of peanut butter, or maybe try a La Tur, a mild, mixed-milk, Italian bloomy-rinded cheese that is often considered the "ice cream" of the cheese world. Pretend you're drinking a bourbon county milkshake—or just make yourself a Bourbon County Stout milkshake!

BITTER

The word *bitter* has a bad reputation, but bitterness serves as a great balancing partner. Hops don't just balance the sweetness of the malts and other flavors in beer—they can do the same for food (see page 68).

Pairing Tip Hop-forward beers tend to work well with their opposites: salty-sweet-smoky foods (think barbecue), fat-rich dishes (salmon), umami flavors (mushrooms), and even some desserts. As a general rule, the more hop-forward the beer, the bolder the ingredients and cooking techniques in the dish can be.

Rule Breaker When bitterness is bold, as in an Imperial IPA, the beer will either work extremely well in a slam-dunk pairing or completely clash with other flavors. An IPA with dark chocolate is a good example of a pairing that tends to take the bitterness in both to unpalatable levels (for more on beer and chocolate pairings, see page 194).

Classic Pub fare (fish and chips), grilled and salt-cured meats (corned beef, ham, pastrami), fried chicken, salted nuts

Other Pâtés, creamy pastas, Indian curries, Chinese salmon, artichokes, mushrooms, carrot cake

The Illinois, Goose IPA, Green Line, and select limited releases

SPICY

Heat-centric spices and peppers are firing up everything from street food bites to fine dining dishes. That's good news for beer, an excellent pairing choice with spicy foods.

The heat sensation in certain spices is amplified by wines that are high in tannins, while both delicate and more complex wines can easily be overpowered by spices. Sweeter wines like Riesling tend to be the go-to pairings with spicy dishes, but beer is a more balanced pairing choice.

Pairing Tip Balanced, crisp pale ales like 312 Urban Wheat Ale are refreshing palate cleansers with spicy food, while medium-bodied Belgian-style ales like Matilda can cut through the heat with their subtle tanginess.

IPA with Caution (or Abandon) Like tannins, bitterness increases the perceived sensation of heat.* Still, IPAs and similar beers make great spicy food flavor partners.

For a heat-wary crowd, go with a less hop-driven beer. For those with a higher heat tolerance, an Imperial IPA or other hops-driven beer may be in order. In fact, that's happening right now: chili heads and IPA geeks have united to conduct unofficial studies at beer and chili pepper events, where the heat-bitterness amplification theory is tested on brave volunteers. Set up a tasting and let us know how it goes. @Goose_Island #bravery

Exceptions: If the beer also has a high alcohol content, the spiciness of the food and the perceived bitterness in the beer both skyrocket.

*Spicy-heat is not the same as a spicy dish loaded with savory spices like cumin, coriander, and similar, as in curries. That creeping, sudden hot burn on your fingers after chopping a hot pepper is the physical sensation caused by hot ingredients activating nerves that are not connected to the taste buds. Hop-forward beers like IPAs often pair very well with dishes that are loaded with taste bud-activated spices, including many Indian dishes—especially when they aren't loaded with hot peppers or spices like cayenne.

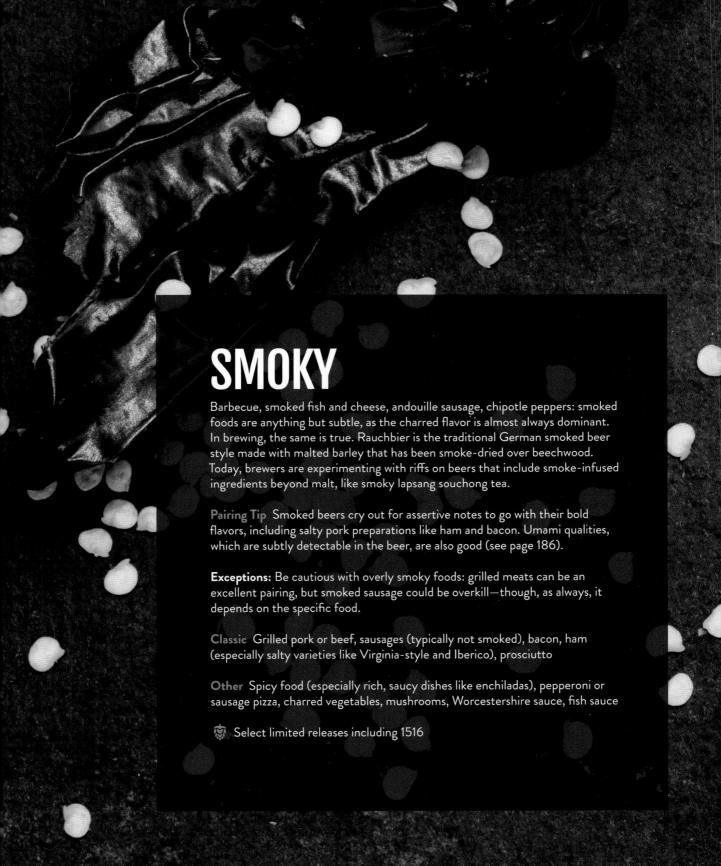

SMOKY

Barbecue, smoked fish and cheese, andouille sausage, chipotle peppers: smoked foods are anything but subtle, as the charred flavor is almost always dominant. In brewing, the same is true. Rauchbier is the traditional German smoked beer style made with malted barley that has been smoke-dried over beechwood. Today, brewers are experimenting with riffs on beers that include smoke-infused ingredients beyond malt, like smoky lapsang souchong tea.

Pairing Tip Smoked beers cry out for assertive notes to go with their bold flavors, including salty pork preparations like ham and bacon. Umami qualities, which are subtly detectable in the beer, are also good (see page 186).

Exceptions: Be cautious with overly smoky foods: grilled meats can be an excellent pairing, but smoked sausage could be overkill—though, as always, it depends on the specific food.

Classic Grilled pork or beef, sausages (typically not smoked), bacon, ham (especially salty varieties like Virginia-style and Iberico), prosciutto

Other Spicy food (especially rich, saucy dishes like enchiladas), pepperoni or sausage pizza, charred vegetables, mushrooms, Worcestershire sauce, fish sauce

🍺 Select limited releases including 1516

UMAMI

If anything, the word umami is obscure. Not exactly a flavor, aroma, or mouthfeel, more a combination of all three, umami is technically derived from the amino acid glutamate.

Sometimes the umami experience comes from a single ingredient, like soy sauce or good old MSG (monosodium glutamate). In some foods, like Parmesan cheese, the longer the cheese is aged, the more umami is detectable. Just as often, umami is a combination of foods and/or beverages working together, as in miso soup (miso, kombu, bonito flakes). Confused? Maybe the inability to describe the "sixth sense" is part of the allure. Time to get tasting.

UMAMI
Food Powerhouses

Asian condiments (miso, soy sauce, fish sauce, bonito flakes), cooked tomatoes (paste, ketchup), cured fish (anchovies, other salt-cured fish), fresh oysters, aged cheeses (Parmesan), cured meats (salami, prosciutto, ham, traditional sausage), barbecue, mushrooms (full-flavored fresh and dried ones), dried seaweed (kombu, kelp), bone-based broths, yeast (especially wild)

AN UMAMI PROST!

At the Chicago launch party for 1516, our fall 2016 Fulton & Wood release (see page 146), we served food that did double-duty as a toast to Germany; the beer was named in honor of the 500th anniversary of the German Purity Law. The lineup included traditional German sausages, a whole roast pig (in other words, ham), and plenty of chubby, freshly baked pretzels. The unexpected food pairing benefit? The ale's subtle smokiness, bready-malt qualities, and other umami-leaning tendencies were suddenly front and center in between each salty, meaty, and yeasty bite.

Umami in Beer

Yeast

It's no coincidence that yeast is used to make many umami-rich foods. Those foods in which the yeast is used for fermentation, as opposed to leavening as with baking, tend to be the most umami-rich. While all beers are fermented, those with a particularly "yeasty" quality tend to be wild yeast-fermented ales and similar styles.

Other Ingredients In any well-crafted beer, be on the lookout for umami lurking unexpectedly around the corner. Smoke is a good example. On its own, the quality isn't typically considered overly umami-like. But a complex beer brewed with smoked hops or other ingredients, like a traditional Bavarian-style Rauch-Kellerbier made with malts smoked with beechwood, might invoke the sixth sense if it also has enough yeasty, malty, or other umami-friendly components (for more on smoked beer, see page 185).

Want to go even further? Experiment with grilled meats—barbecue party!—or umami-leaning vegetables like fresh mushrooms or truffles.

Aging A chunk of aged Parmesan, a plate full of slow-smoked barbecue. Good things come to those who wait. Big, malty, barrel-aged beers like Bourbon County Brand Stout that are aged for a long period of time can also take on subtler umami-like qualities.

This is one reason why lining up five annual vintages of Bourbon County Brand Stout can get really interesting, and sometimes almost too complex to describe ... not unlike the word umami.

TART

Sour cherries, grapefruit, Greek yogurt, sauerkraut. Tart flavors in beer have pleasantly acidic qualities similar to many tart foods. In a beer, the flavors can run from moderately sour—think Sofie, a beer with almost Champagne-like qualities—to bold and funky, like the Sour Sisters. Each beer develops a unique complexity from wild yeast fermentation, barrel aging, and, in many cases, additional ingredients like fresh fruit.

Pairing Tip Take a cue from the food world, where sour flavors are often balanced with sweet flavors (balsamic vinaigrettes, sweet and sour chicken). Sour ales typically contrast well with saltiness or bitterness and cut the "fattiness" in rich foods like eggs and shellfish.

Tangy and Delicate

Classic Rich shellfish (lobster, scallops with cream sauce, mussels), egg dishes (poached eggs, frittatas)

Other Crab, mild seafood (white fish, sushi), arugula or frisée salad, citrus tarts

 Sofie and select limited releases, including Caution Tape

Tart and Bold

Classic Pâtés, moules frites (steamed mussels and fries), fruit sauces and jams (apple, fig, pear), waffles

Other Foie gras, sugar-cured meat sauces (balsamic, gastrique, brown sugar), roast turkey, pork, dark chocolate, cheesecake

 The Sour Sisters (Gillian, Halia, Juliet, Lolita, and Madame Rose) and select limited releases, including Lilith

SWEET

Beer can be an excellent—and unexpected—dessert choice at a tasting dinner. Dry, tannic wines typically don't work well with sweet flavors. On the opposite end, sweet or fortified wines can feel like an old-school choice that younger drinkers might not consider. Sparkling wine can be a good match ... if only backtracking to lighter wines after a multi-course meal didn't require taste bud gymnastics.

With beer, the beverage can be as creative and experimental as the final course.

Variety Styles of beer are so varied, from lighter beers to big, port-like aged stouts, that the pairing options are virtually limitless. Nutty, spicy, citrusy, fruity (berries, cherries, peaches, and other fruits), creamy, chocolate, and caramel desserts can all find the right beer match. Incredibly complex beers, like Bourbon County Brand Coffee Stout, can serve as dessert on their own or, with a few tweaks, become a drink and dessert in one, as in the affogato on page 191.

Pairing Tip Sugar is a powerful palate rush. In general, choose higher ABV (6% and above) beers to match desserts. Most higher ABV beers still clock in at a much lower alcohol level than most dessert wines, a bonus for multi-course tastings when controlling the amount of alcohol may become an issue.

Exceptions: With sweetness in particular, avoid palate overkill by bringing in opposite flavors at the same time.

Sweet Pairings

Several styles of beer and desserts share flavor components that work well together. Honkers Ale paired with pecan pie? Hello, classic Thanksgiving dessert-pairing solution. Looking for something unexpected? Certain contrasting beer and dessert styles can make some of the best and most surprising pairings—think Goose IPA and carrot cake with cream cheese frosting.

Malty Ales
Warm spices (cinnamon, clove, nutmeg), toasted nuts, caramel

Flavor Parallels Apple pie, gingerbread, nut pies and tarts, oatmeal cookies, bread pudding, flan

Flavor Opposites Pungent blue cheeses like Maytag Blue or Stilton
Golden Rule Caveat Very sweet desserts paired with malty beers can sometimes accentuate the bitterness of a beer or create the perception that the dessert is too sweet.

Sour, Fruity Ales
Tangy, fruity, citrusy

Flavor Parallels Fruit-based desserts that complement the fruit in the beer
Flavor Opposites Cream-rich desserts or accents (ice cream, puddings, custards, cream sauces), cheesecakes with complementary fruit sauces
Golden Rule Caveat Acidic beers cut through creamy desserts with fruity accents, but they can also add an unwanted astringency to already acidic desserts.

Hop-Forward Beers
Bitterness offsets fat and sugar

Flavor Parallels Citrusy and herbaceous
Flavor Opposites Cream cheese (carrot cake), ice cream, and similar
Golden Rule Caveat The bitterness in very dark chocolate can increase the bitterness in hop-forward beers to the point where the combination is unpalatable; in other cases, chocolate can work surprisingly well.

Barrel-Aged Stouts like Bourbon County Brand Stout
Rich flavors, intense complexity

Flavor Parallels Dark chocolate (for more on chocolate pairings, see page 194), coffee
Flavor Opposites Berries, dark cherry, stone fruit
Golden Rule Caveat These styles of beer have a tendency to overpower nuanced desserts. Citrus (sorbet, lemon tart) and sour dairy (frozen yogurt) flavors often clash.

CANDYLAND

Chicago was once the candy capital of the world, with Henry Heide Candy Company leading the pack in the 1860s, followed by Brach's Candies, Curtis Candy Company, Farley Candy Company, Ferrara Pan Company, Bob's Candies, Slathers Candy Company, and many more. Several candy factories still operate in and around the Chicago area.

Got a beer and candy pairing idea? Baby Ruth, Boston Baked Beans, Butterfinger, candy corn, caramels, Cracker Jacks, Lemonheads, Snickers, and Tootsie Rolls are just a few of the candies that have Chicago ties. @Goose_Island #gimmecandy

BOURBON COUNTY AFFOGATO RECIPE

Place two small scoops of ice cream (coffee, chocolate, or vanilla) in a coffee cup (preferably a fancy one), then pour a shot of Bourbon County Brand Stout or Bourbon County Brand Coffee Stout on top and garnish with shaved dark chocolate, and *voilà,* dessert is served.

Complementary "Sweet" Flavors in Desserts & Beer
Monday-morning pairing moment? Every beer has a unique complexity, so we don't like to use the term "never fail." Still, these beer and dessert pairings typically do work well together.

DESSERT PAIRING GUIDE

DESSERT INGREDIENT / TYPE	DOMINANT FLAVORS	BEERS
Caramel, honey, maple syrup	Toasted malt, buttery-sweet	Honkers Ale, Oktoberfest, Matilda, Winter Ale, F&W Bee Squad, Pere Jacques
Cookies and cake (vanilla, oatmeal and similar), cream-based desserts (cheesecake, crème brûlée, ice cream, pudding)	Creamy and malty, marshmallow-sweet	Honkers Ale, Matilda, F&W Fassinator, F&W Rasselbock, Pere Jacques, Bourbon County Brand Stout
Coffee, chocolate (for more on chocolate, see page 194)	Bittersweet, complex	Winter Ale, Bourbon County Brand Stout, Bourbon County Coffee Stout, F&W 1516, Fulton Street Blend Coffee Ale, Pepe Nero
Nuts, warm spices (cinnamon, clove, licorice, nutmeg, star anise)	Toasty, spicy	Honkers Ale, Oktoberfest, Winter Ale, F&W Von Kaiser, F&W Rasselbock
Apples	Tart, fruity	312 Urban Wheat Ale, Sofie, Honkers Ale
Apricots, peaches, pears	Floral, delicate	Halia, Sofie, Goose IPA, The Ogden, F&W Bee Squad, F&W Von Kaiser
Cherries, berries	Liqueur-like, tangy-sweet	Gillian, Lolita, Juliet, Madame Rose, Bourbon County Brand Stout
Lemons, limes, oranges	Citrusy, bright	Sofie, Green Line, Summertime Kölsch, F&W C.A.L.M. Radler
Dried fruit	Earthy, complex (aged)	Juliet, Madame Rose, Bourbon County Brand Barleywine
Cheese		See Cheese, pages 180–182

MALTY

All beer is "malty" to some extent. Like hops, malt is a fundamental brewing ingredient, but only beers with pronounced "malty" flavors in the finished beer—nutty, toasty, roasted, caramel, and similar—are typically described as malty. Beers that have predominantly sweet flavors from residual malt sugars not consumed by yeast or a high alcohol content (without hop balance) are also described as "malty." Some beers have subtler malt flavor characteristics, like Honkers Ale, while others, like those in the Bourbon County Series, can be so robust and malty that they have earned their own flavor category.

Pairing Tip Beers that fall into the classic "malty" spectrum typically work well with a broad range of foods. The balanced sweetness acts as an excellent balance for salty foods, as in the classic Irish stout and oyster pairing, or Fest Bier with traditional brats and pretzels.

The unique flavor and aroma profiles among richer, barrel-aged stouts invite unique food pairing opportunities, again (you know this part!) depending on the specific beer. In general, foods that work well are bold without overshadowing the beer's complexity, from grilled steak to dark chocolate.

Malty
Classic Cured meats, roasted pork and poultry, oysters, toasted nuts
Other Wild game, caramel, coffee, chocolate

 Fest Bier, Winter Ale, Pere Jacques, and select limited releases including Rasselbock

Malty & Robust
Classic Grilled steak, dark chocolate, toasted nuts
Other Coffee, toffee, maple syrup, other flavor parallels in the beer

 Bourbon County Brand Stout series and select limited releases

BCBS
Flavor Diversity
Beers in the original Bourbon County Brand Stout series pick up parallel nuances directly from the former whiskey aging barrels (vanilla, oak, charred, and—of course—bourbon notes). Bourbon County Brand Coffee Stout clearly has more intense coffee flavors and aromas, while others, like the 2011 Bramble Rye Bourbon County Stout, develop fruity flavors from ingredients like Michigan raspberries and blackberries. The 2016 Bourbon County Brand Stout Proprietor's Blend, which included chipotle peppers and was aged in barrels that previously held maple syrup, went in an entirely different layered flavor direction.

Good-quality **dark chocolate** is typically a unifying pairing force for these richly flavored, barrel-aged stouts. Chocolate tends to have a similarly broad range of flavor nuances, from fruity to smoky, that work well with them (for more on beer and chocolate, see page 194).

CHOCOLATE

Beer and chocolate? Yes. Really. Chocolate is one of the most complex, challenging, and—if you hit a sweet spot—incredible pairings with beer. Several beer styles, including stouts and porters, have fundamental flavor profiles—think coffee, toffee, malt, and chocolate—that complement both chocolate bars and sweeter chocolate desserts.

Push the flavor intensity even further with a complex, barrel-aged stout like those in the Bourbon County Brand Stout series. Belgian-style ales and even lighter beers like Saisons can also work with chocolate. Like other foods, it all depends on the flavor combinations.

Dark Chocolate

Pure and lightly sweetened dark chocolates are loaded with complex flavors. The variety of cocoa beans, terroir (location, farming practices, and similar environmental effects), percentage of chocolate to sugar, and skill of the chocolate maker all come into play. Sound familiar? Brewers and artisan chocolatiers run in the same flavor circles—coffee roasters, too (for more on Goose Island's coffee collaborations, see page 137).

White Chocolate

Made from cocoa butter alone, white chocolate does not contain the same complex cocoa derivatives as "real" chocolate. For pairing purposes, white chocolate is more akin to a sugary candy or vanilla frosting. Remember, bitter and sweet are opposite flavor categories, so white chocolate can also work well with bitter beers like double IPAs.

Does your chocolate have...

nutty and toasty "malt" flavors or vanilla notes? Try balanced British or Belgian-style ales, lighter Saisons, blondes, and similar beers with honey, or go the opposite route with malt-rich porters and stouts.
Honkers Ale, Winter Ale, Matilda, Fest Bier, Pere Jacques, Bourbon County Brand Stout, and select limited releases including Fassinator and Bee Squad

coffee or warm spices like cinnamon, clove, and nutmeg? Experiment with spiced ales that mimic those flavors or bigger barrel-aged stouts or porters.
Honkers Ale, Fest Bier, Winter Ale, Bourbon County Brand Coffee Stout, and select limited releases, including Fulton & Wood Von Kaiser

fruity characteristics? Try barrel-aged sour beers with complex, chocolate-friendly fruits like berries or Belgian-style farmhouse ales (Saisons) with citrusy notes.
Juliet (blackberries), Lolita (raspberries), Gillian (strawberries, black pepper), Madame Rose (cherries), Halia (peaches), Sofie (citrus, pepper)

LOVE TRIANGLE

Somewhere in date-night history, wine and dark chocolate became an idealized "romantic" pairing. Like chocolate, wine is high in tannins. Wines that are especially tannic are described as dry, the same quality that lends dark chocolate its signature bitterness. That double hit of bitterness is the same reason very hop-forward beers like IPAs typically don't work with bittersweet chocolate. (Take a sip of a double IPA and a bite of unsweetened chocolate, and you'll know what we mean.) With bitter beers, experiment with milk chocolate or lighter chocolate desserts that have enough sugar and cream to temper the chocolate's bitterness.

Five
"FANCY" FOODS

We've talked about the way that beer has more flavor compounds than wine, but beer still gets the short end of the stick in the fine dining world, with wine being the preferred pairing for some of the world's finest delicacies. Here are five pairings to prove that beer can pair just as beautifully or, dare we say, *better* with some of the best ingredients in the world.

CAVIAR
Pairing Honkers Ale
Why Certain caviars possess full flavors that can be smoky, bready, and even nutty, while most finish slightly sweet and clean. These flavors work perfectly with an amber ale like Honkers, especially caviars and roe like Hackleback, white sturgeon, Russian osetra (farmed), and whitefish roe.

TRUFFLES
Pairing Matilda
Why Fungi that grow on the roots of trees like oak and beech are some of the most sought-after and expensive ingredients in cooking for good reason. Called "the diamond of the kitchen," truffles have incredibly earthy, pungent, and funky flavors. Some have even described those qualities as animal musk. Matilda, a Belgian-style ale with notes of earth, cedar, and horse blanket (in a good way), is the perfect pairing for all types of truffles.

FOIE GRAS
Paring Gillian
Why To some, foie gras is the "essence of umami" (for more on umami, see page 186). This fat-rich goose liver treat has deep flavor notes reminiscent of beef marrow and is massively (literally!) creamy, soft, and melty on the palate. Gillian acts like a strawberry and white pepper gastrique that complements the richness of foie gras with notes of sweet acidity.

KOBE BEEF
Pairing Goose IPA
Why The cows that this exquisite beef comes from are a Tajima-ushi breed of Wagyu cattle and are raised in the Hyogo prefecture in Japan. They are fed with beer (!!!) and grain and are massaged (yes, by real people) to ensure optimal tenderness. The result is a rich, fatty beef that can rival foie gras for that melt-in-your-mouth factor. The big hop profile in Goose IPA is what makes this a perfect pairing, as the herbaceous notes of pine and citrus combined with the dry, bitter finish contrast perfectly with this style of beef. Or, who knows ... maybe it's because of the beer the cattle drank.

TORO
Pairing Four Star Pils
Why The best and most desirable part of the tuna belly is toro, specifically otoro. This cut is the fattiest part of the fish, which causes it to melt in your mouth. Toro needs something crisp and clean with a solid hop backbone to help cut through that fat and get the palate ready for another bite. Four Star Pils does that perfectly. The beer is nuanced enough in flavor to not overpower the subtle flavors in the tuna.

RECIPES
Brewing *Is* Cooking

At Goose Island, the ingredients we put in each beer are the best we can find. That's true whether the endgame is a classic Imperial IPA or an experimental Fulton & Wood beer that's limited only by our brewers' imaginations. We cook with the same mindset, whether we're on the hunt for an authentic Chicago dog (neon-green relish and all) or a dish that combines spices and other ingredients in an unfamiliar way. Maybe that's why cooking with beer pairings in mind is one of the most gratifying experiences—or, fine, it just tastes d@#% good.

The recipes on the following pages have been handed down by our brewers, staff, local chefs, and even our fans. Try a few, create your own, and share the tasting results: @Goose_Island. Cheers!

Barley-based beer has been around since ancient times, and surely, so have barley griddle cakes of some kind, so we'll say that's why we included this recipe. (Really, we just wanted a reason to say that Sumerians invented the straw around 2400 BC as a way to drink beer without stirring up the sediment on the bottom. How cool is that?) Unlike the sprouted malted barley used in brewing, barley flour is toasted before milling so the earthy flavors really come to the forefront. The balsamic vinegar gives the cherry compote enough heft to rally into the world of appetizers (goat cheese), mains (pork chops or duck sauce), and dessert (ice cream).

Toss all of the waffle ingredients into a bowl the night before so you're ready to roll in the morning, or do it while the coffee brews before work. Or if it's been *that* kind of day and you want to keep it simple, maple syrup is a fine substitute for the Cherry-Orange Compote. (Although you can make the compote far in advance, and it's mighty handy to have around.)

Brewer's
WAFFLES
Cherry-Orange Compote, Whipped Mascarpone

1½ cups buttermilk or whole milk

4 tablespoons (2 ounces) unsalted butter

¼ cup honey

½ cup rolled oats, regular or instant

1½ cups whole wheat flour

1 cup barley flour

2¼ teaspoons (1 packet) instant or active dry yeast

½ teaspoon kosher salt, or to taste

3 large eggs, lightly beaten

FOR SERVING

Melted butter (optional, but good), Cherry-Orange Compote & Whipped Mascarpone (recipes follow), zest of a small orange (optional)

Makes 4 large waffles (or more with smaller waffle irons)

BATTER

In a medium saucepan over low heat, warm the milk, ⅓ cup water, butter, and honey until the butter and honey melt; set aside. In a blender, grind the oats until fine and add to a large bowl with the whole wheat and barley flours, yeast, and salt. Use a fork to stir the warm milk mixture into the flours, then stir in the eggs. (See how easy this is without caffeine?) Cover the bowl with plastic wrap and refrigerate overnight or up to 12 hours. Or, let the batter rise in a warm spot for 1½ to 2 hours until it is bubbly and smells nice and yeasty.

WAFFLES

Heat a waffle iron as directed, typically medium to medium-high heat. Preheat the oven to 250°F to keep the waffles warm, or use a toaster. When the waffle iron is hot, add the recommended amount of batter; for large waffle irons, use about 1 cup of batter per waffle. Close the iron (don't peek!), and cook for a solid 2 to 3 minutes before lifting the lid. The waffle should be golden brown and firm; if not, cook it a little longer. Keep the waffles warm in the oven while you cook the remaining ones.

CHERRY-ORANGE COMPOTE

Pit about 1½ pounds (4 cups) fresh **cherries**. Mix the cherries, a finger-size strip of **orange peel**, ½ cup freshly squeezed **orange juice**, 3 tablespoons **balsamic vinegar**, and ⅓ cup **sugar** in a medium nonreactive saucepan (choose one with high sides, as this tends to boil over easily). Bring the liquid to a boil, reduce to a simmer, and stir every so often. Cook the cherries until the sauce darkens to a ruby color and reduces slightly, usually a solid 15 minutes. The compote will thicken more as it cools. Remove the pan from the heat and add a splash more balsamic vinegar and sugar, if you'd like. Cool the compote completely, remove the orange peel, and refrigerate for up to 2 weeks. Makes about 3 cups.

FOR THE WHIPPED MASCARPONE

Let a container of **mascarpone** (8 ounces/1 cup) warm up on the counter for about 30 minutes. Whip the mascarpone, along with a spoonful of **maple syrup**, if you'd like, in a stand mixer with the paddle attachment until fluffy. Or, if you have the patience, you can whip the mascarpone by hand (a large spoon works best). Makes 1 generous cup.

SERVE

Put the waffles on serving plates and drizzle some melted butter on top. Spoon the cherry compote generously over each, give each a dollop of mascarpone, and sprinkle a little orange zest on top. Even better, let everyone build their own waffles.

PAIRS WITH
SOFIE
SOFIE-MOSA
COCKTAIL
MADAME ROSE
see p. 212

BEER COCKTAILS

The taste is unmistakably modern, with layers of sophisticated flavors, but beer cocktails have been around since at least the 1850s. The first British "shandy gaffs" (today called shandys) were made with a mixture of beer and ginger ale; German tavern owners began mixing up radlers, a Bavarian twist with lemonade to stretch the offerings when beer supplies were running low.

Today, brewers recreate similar flavors in bottled beers, as in Goose Island's C.A.L.M Radler (see page 145), and beer cocktails are also making a comeback. Some, like the Sofie-Mosa, are refreshingly lower in alcohol than standard cocktails, which is a nice feature at any time of day.

SOFIE-MOSA

An easy, elegant, and refreshingly unexpected twist on a mimosa. Vary the citrus with cara cara oranges or tangerines, or use blood orange juice for color. Use a large chalice or similarly shaped glass, or reduce the quantity to fit a Champagne flute.

Pour 3 ounces **fresh orange juice** into a chalice or Goose Vintage Glassware. Top with 5 ounces well-chilled Sofie. Garnish with an **orange twist**.

For a brunch crowd, the ratio is 15 ounces of orange juice for every 765ml bottle (25.8 ounces) of Sofie. Pour both into a pitcher just before serving. Each bottle makes 5 cocktails.

FLEUR DE SAISON (SEASONAL FLOWER)

French liqueur and Sofie make for a sophisticated pair in this updated variation on a sparkling wine cocktail.

Pour ½ ounce **St. Germain** elderflower liqueur in a Champagne flute and top with 6 ounces Sofie. Garnish with a **candied orange peel**.

PIMM'S IPA

In this spin on the summery English classic, Goose IPA stands in for the traditional lemonade or more bracing ginger beer.

Pour 1 ounce **Pimm's No. 1** into a highball glass filled only halfway with ice. Gently rub 2 to 3 small **mint leaves** between your fingers briefly to release the oils. Put the mint leaves and 1 thin **cucumber** slice (unpeeled, any variety) in the glass, fill with more ice, and top off with 5 to 6 ounces Goose IPA. Garnish with a mint sprig and slice of cucumber.

URBAN GINGER

Traditional ginger beer takes on a new meaning in this beer cocktail.

Combine 1 ounce **Domaine de Canton** ginger liqueur and ½ ounce (2 tablespoons) **fresh lemon juice** in an ice-filled cocktail shaker. Slowly pour 5 ounces 312 Urban Wheat Ale down the side of the shaker. When the foam subsides, gently stir and pour the mixture into an ice-filled highball glass. Garnish with a **candied ginger strip**.

C.A.L.M. DAIQUIRI

A tribute to beer cocktail history, this herbaceous and effervescent twist on the daiquiri uses Goose Island's very own version of a radler.

Combine 1 ounce **fresh lime juice,** ¼ ounce **simple syrup,** 1¼ ounces **white rum,** and 1 ounce **Pimm's No. 1** in an ice-filled cocktail shaker. Shake like crazy for a minute or two, strain into a chalice or martini glass, and top with 4 ounces C.A.L.M. Radler. Garnish with a **lime wedge**.

MATILDA SPIKED CIDER

The cold-weather warmer gets an update for those who migrate to—or are lucky enough to live at—the beach during the holiday season.

Core and cut 1 unpeeled, sweet **apple** (Honey Crisp, Pink Lady, or similar) into small chunks. In a cocktail shaker, muddle together 1 ounce **honey**, slightly warmed, with the apple until the fruit is nicely smashed. Fill the shaker with ice, add 3 ounces **fresh apple cider**, 1 ounce **bourbon**, and the juice of 1 small **lemon wedge**. Pour in 2 to 3 ounces Matilda, to taste. Stir well, and strain into an ice-filled rocks glass. Garnish with a pinch of **ground allspice**.

MATILDA APPLE TODDY

In Chicago, winter beach envy doesn't keep us from brewing—and surfing—in twenty-degree weather. Besides, we know this hot toddy will be waiting.

Brew a teacup-size batch of English Breakfast or similar **black tea**. Pour 4 ounces of tea into a large mug (drink the rest). Stir in 1 teaspoon **honey** and 1 scant tablespoon (about 1 ounce) **apple butter**, more to taste. Top with 6 ounces Matilda (room temperature) and garnish with a pinch of **fresh nutmeg**.

Bulgogi
BREAKFAST TACOS
Fried Eggs, Quick Pickled Red Onions, Red Chile–Tomatillo Salsa

1½ to 2 pounds flank steak or similar

⅓ cup soy sauce

¼ cup Honkers Ale or similar

3 tablespoons brown sugar, packed

1 tablespoon toasted sesame oil

3 garlic cloves, minced

1 teaspoon grated ginger

2 scallions, thinly sliced halfway up the green stem

2 tablespoons sesame seeds

¼ teaspoon red pepper flakes, more to taste

1 teaspoon freshly ground black pepper

Vegetable oil and unsalted butter, for cooking

6 eggs

FOR SERVING

Flour tortillas (for 6 tacos plus extras for sopping), Red Chile–Tomatillo Salsa, Quick Pickled Red Onions (recipes follow), 1 bunch roughly chopped cilantro

BEEF MARINADE

Trim any large pieces of fat from the beef. Very thinly slice the beef into thin pieces across the grain. Stir together the soy sauce, beer, brown sugar, sesame oil, garlic, ginger, scallions, sesame seeds, and both peppers in a medium bowl. Toss the meat in the marinade, cover, and refrigerate for about 1 hour.

TACOS

Strain the beef and lightly dry the slices on paper towels. Heat a little oil in a large skillet until very hot. Pan-fry the beef a few slices at a time, flipping once, until medium rare, about 1 minute if the slices are very thin. The cooking time will vary depending on how thinly you sliced the beef. You want a nice sear on the meat, so try not to overcrowd the pan.

FOR THE QUICK PICKLED RED ONIONS

Thinly slice 1 large **red onion,** put the slices in a medium bowl, and pour ½ cup boiling water on top. Strain immediately, and rinse the onions in cold water. In the same bowl, whisk together ½ cup **unseasoned rice vinegar,** ½ cup water, and ½ teaspoon each of **sugar** and **kosher salt.** Marinate the onions for 1 to 2 hours, if you are up early enough. Strain and use right away, or refrigerate for a few hours.

FOR THE RED CHILE–TOMATILLO SALSA

De-stem and scrape the seeds from 2 **dried ancho chiles** (often mistakenly labeled pasillas). Toast the chiles in a large, dry cast-iron skillet over high heat until blackened in spots. Submerge the chiles in a bowl of warm water and set aside. Husk, rinse, and dry 1 pound of **tomatillos.** In the same skillet, dry-sear the tomatillos and 5 large **garlic cloves** (unpeeled), turning often until blackened and soft, about 10 minutes. Cover, and let the tomatillos soften up for another few minutes. Drain the ancho chiles and transfer with the tomatillos and garlic (squeeze the cloves out of the skins) to a blender or food processor. Add ½ teaspoon each **sugar** and **kosher salt** and a nice pour (about ¼ cup) of a **citrusy ale** like Sofie. Puree the salsa until chunky or smooth—whatever you like—and season with salt to taste. Use immediately, or refrigerate for up to 5 days. Makes 1 generous cup.

SERVE

Have all of your taco components ready: tortillas (toasted in a dry skillet, if you'd like), salsa, pickled onions, and chopped cilantro. Melt a pat of butter in a large nonstick or heavy-bottomed sauté pan and fry the eggs sunny side up so the yolks are still runny. Season with salt and pepper.

Lay 6 tortillas on serving plates and pile some beef on each, then slide an egg on top. Drizzle a spoonful or two of the salsa on top and tuck a few pickled onions alongside the other fillings. Top the tacos with cilantro and put the extra salsa and pickled onions on the table. Put any extra beef on the table for round two, and then hurry up and sit down with a good beer to eat them.

PAIRS WITH
312 URBAN WHEAT
4 STAR PILS

This recipe from Jesse Valenciana, our go-to for Goose Migration Weeks and other events, is a cultural mash-up built around bulgogi-style seared beef (Korean), pickled red onions (German, Eastern European... modern urban homesteader?), and a red chile sauce freshened up with tomatillos (Tex-Mex, Cal-Mex).

Jesse stuffs everything inside flour tortillas made with bacon fat instead of shortening; check out his cookbook, *ManBQue*, for the recipe. Store-bought flour tortillas are a fine substitute. A river of egg yolks has a way of making everything taste great at any time of day.

We love salt-cured fish. It can be as fancy or down-home as you'd like, and the salt and herbs do all of the work while you figure out what beer you might serve at the unveiling. Pop open a vintage bottle or go with something more refreshing.

The steelhead used in this recipe is a variety of rainbow trout with the flavor qualities and color of salmon that migrates from rivers to the Great Lakes or oceans. The fish is farmed in the United States, including by our neighbors in Lake Michigan. It typically arrives super fresh to retail shops within a day or two of harvesting, which is essential for making cured fish. (Don't use previously frozen fish or fresh fish that is past its prime.) Most commercial steelhead is already deboned, but you can pull out any bones with tweezers if needed (if you caught one yourself, congratulations). Slice a few radishes and pull out the good grainy mustard and the cornichons—tiny pickles!

Herb-Cured
GRAVLAX
Ginger, Dill, Coriander, Lemon

1 steelhead trout fillet (skin on), about 1½ pounds, deboned

3 tablespoons kosher salt, divided

1 tablespoon sugar

1 large or 2 small bunches dill, tough bottom stems discarded

1 leafy bunch parsley, tough bottom stems discarded

½ large red onion, cut into large chunks

3-inch nub ginger, peeled and sliced into thin coins

1 teaspoon ground coriander

Juice of 2 large lemons, more if needed

FOR SERVING

Lemon wedges, grainy mustard, cornichons, rye or other crackers, and thinly sliced radishes or cucumbers, if you'd like

Makes 8 appetizer servings, more if part of a cocktail party buffet spread

FISH CURE

Rinse the fish in cold running water and pat dry with paper towels. Place an extra-long piece of plastic wrap lengthwise in a glass or ceramic baking dish large enough for the fish to lay flat. The plastic wrap should hang over both ends by a few inches. Lay two more pieces of plastic wrap width-wise across the dish. Lay the fish fillet in the dish and lightly rub 1½ tablespoons of salt on the flesh side and the remaining 1½ tablespoons of salt on the opposite side with skin. Don't be tempted to skimp on the salt; it cures the fish.

Put the remaining ingredients—sugar, dill, parsley, red onion, ginger, coriander, and lemon juice—in a high-speed blender or food processor. Puree everything into a paste. If needed, add another squeeze or two of lemon juice to get things going.

Spoon about half of the herb paste all over one side of the fish and put the fish, paste-side down, in the prepared dish. Coat the top with the remaining herb paste and seal up the fish in the plastic wrap, tucking in the edges snugly like a mummy so the juices stay put. Place a heavy pot or baking pan on top of the fish, place cans of food inside it for more weight, and refrigerate for 24 hours, then flip the fillet over so the opposite side is facing up. Refrigerate for another 24 to 48 hours for a total curing time of 2 to 3 days.

SERVE

Unwrap the fish and rinse quickly in cold water to remove most of the herb paste. Pat dry and carefully remove the skin with a sharp knife. Serve the fish right away, or cover and refrigerate for up to 2 days. Slice the fish thinly across the grain and serve with the lemon wedges, grainy mustard, pickles, rye or other crackers, and whatever else suits your cured mood.

PAIRS WITH
312 URBAN WHEAT
C.A.L.M. RADLER
SUMMERTIME KÖLSCH
SOFIE

5 to 6 mixed citrus fruits (more if very small, like blood oranges, mandarins, or similar)

1 chubby, tangy-sweet grapefruit, like Ruby Red

½ medium red onion

1 large avocado

FOR SERVING

Castelvetrano olives (10-ounce jar, about 1 cup, drained), shelled unsalted pistachios (small handful), sea salt, freshly ground pepper, avocado oil or good olive oil

SALAD PREP

Peel and slice the citrus, including the grapefruit, into thin wheels. Pop out and discard any seeds and pithy centers. Use the citrus right away or chill for up to 12 hours. Very thinly slice the red onion and soak the slices in ice water for several minutes; drain.

SERVE

Arrange the citrus slices on a large serving platter or individual plates. Scatter the drained red onions on top. Slice the avocado in half, lengthwise, remove the pit, and then slice each half into thin wedges. Use a large spoon to scoop the flesh out of each half, then fan out the slices on the plates. Sprinkle sea salt lightly over the salad, add a few grinds of pepper, and scatter the olives and pistachios on top. Finish with a light drizzle of avocado oil or good olive oil.

Sicilian-Style
CITRUS SALAD
Shaved Red Onions, Avocados, Castelvetrano Olives, Pistachios

Something happens when a handful of humble ingredients—winter citrus, shaved red onion, fresh olives, avocado, and good drizzling oil—comes together in an entirely unexpected way. Whoever first put these salad ingredients together would be great at brewing beer. More improvisation than precise recipe, this salad makes for a great Italian-inspired weeknight side dish and is equally impressive at a dinner-party spread. And it's ridiculously easy to make.

You can peel and slice the fruit ahead and pop it in the fridge for several hours, then simply scatter everything on a large serving platter or plates—no tossing required. Castelvetranos are bright green, lightly salt-cured olives with a fresh flavor and buttery texture, the polar opposite of most table olives (skip the olives altogether if you can't find them). Look for them at the olive bar or find jarred versions in the pickle aisle.

PAIRS WITH
HALIA
SOFIE
312 URBAN WHEAT

Chicken
SHIO RAMEN

Shio Broth, Beer-Cured Ajitsuke Eggs

¼ cup sesame oil

1 medium onion, roughly chopped

2-inch piece ginger, peeled and
sliced into thin coins

8 to 10 garlic cloves, peeled and smashed

3 pounds bony chicken parts (back, feet,
wings or similar)

1-ounce package (about 1 generous cup)
dried shiitake mushrooms

1 sheet kombu, roughly the
size of your palm

2 cups loosely packed bonito flakes

2 or more teaspoons togarashi, to taste

2 tablespoons mirin

1 tablespoon unseasoned
rice wine vinegar

1 tablespoon soy sauce

1 tablespoon kosher salt

1 teaspoon white pepper

FOR SERVING

Thin Japanese noodles (ramen, udon, or similar; 1 ounce per serving), Beer-Cured Ajitsuke Eggs (recipe follows; 1 egg per serving), and whatever toppings you like: thinly sliced scallions, watercress, bean sprouts, pickled mushrooms, sesame seeds, and/or meats like pork chashu

Makes about 4 quarts, or 12 to 14 servings

SHIO BROTH

Heat the sesame oil in a large stockpot or Dutch oven over medium-high heat. Add the onion, ginger, and garlic and sauté until nicely browned, stirring regularly. Add a splash of water and scrape the brown bits off the bottom of the pot, then add chicken and 5 quarts of water; 4 quarts is fine if that's all your pot can hold. Stir in the dried shiitakes, kombu, bonito flakes, and 2 to 4 teaspoons togarashi (depending on the heat factor, see next page). Bring the liquid to a boil and keep the broth rolling, uncovered, for 1½ to 2 hours. Let the broth cool.

Strain the broth and press down on the mushrooms to release their flavor. Stir in the mirin, vinegar, soy sauce, kosher salt, and white pepper. Taste, and add more soy sauce, salt, and white pepper if needed. Don't be shy; such a large quantity of stock may need as much as 1 tablespoon of soy sauce and/or salt to get to your umami threshold. Cover and refrigerate the stock to use throughout the upcoming week, or freeze in serving sizes.

FOR THE BEER-CURED AJITSUKE EGGS

Those who soft-boil eggs are an opinionated bunch. (Recipe anxiety spoiler: egg size variations are likely the cause of an over- or undercooked egg.) If you're not married to a certain method, try this one. The soy sauce is the dominant flavor; use any leftover, light- to medium-bodied ale, or even a pilsner. The eggs are great on their own for lunch, too.

continued on page 215

PAIRS WITH
GOOSE IPA
GREEN LINE
4 STAR PILS

CULTURAL SPICE
Togarashi is a savory Japanese spice blend made of red chile peppers ground with dried orange peel, seaweed, ginger, and other spices. Like any spice mix, the heat factor can vary from balanced to nearly as spicy as pure cayenne pepper. Until you get to know your togarashi, start with a conservative amount. This recipe already has plenty of seaweed and ginger, so if you can't find togarashi, substitute ½ to 1 teaspoon of cayenne pepper, to taste, and toss a pinkie-size piece of orange peel in the broth pot.

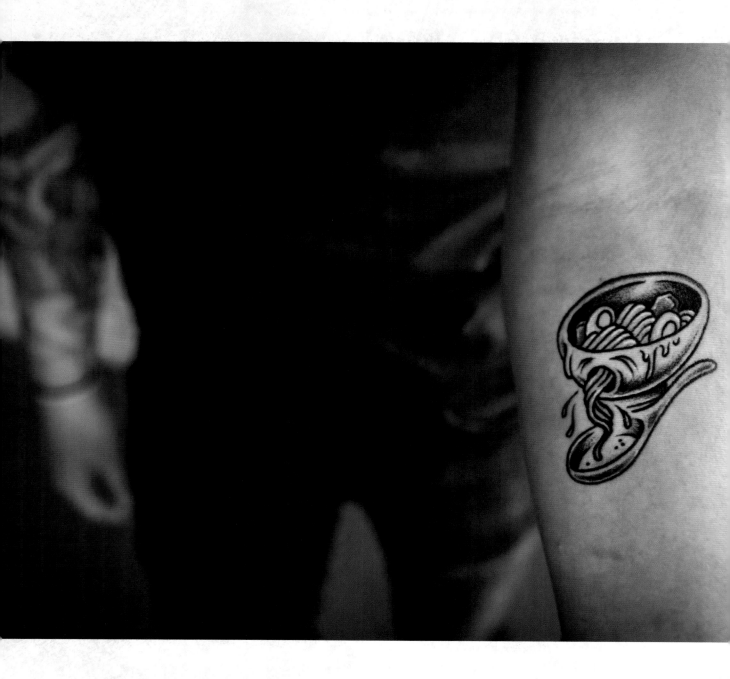

When the office is full of beer lovers and brewers, talk about what's for lunch can get a little out of hand. By mid-afternoon, the food enthusiasm carries over to several company-wide cooking obsessions: pierogies one year, tacos another (for a breakfast taco recipe, see page 206), and lately, ramen. One of our former brewers, Ryan Brei, was so obsessed with ramen that he had a bowl of the Japanese soup tattooed on his arm, complete with a visual slurping design. He makes a big batch of this ramen broth almost every weekend to riff on when he gets home from work. It was somewhat (let's not give him too much of a cooking ego) of a big deal that he shared the recipe with us.

Chicken backs and feet are loaded with gelatin, so you get the signature "slurping" viscosity of a really good ramen broth. Chicken wings also work great. If you can't find good-quality ramen noodles, substitute a good-quality thin Japanese noodle like udon, as we did. (Don't tell Ryan.) Hit a Japanese market for the rest of the ingredients and then, as Ryan says, "Pile on whatever toppings you want...and eat the [a word we can't print] out of it all week."

continued from page 212

Place 8 large or extra-large **eggs** in a medium pot. Submerge the eggs in water by about 1 inch, cover the pot, and crank up the stovetop to very high heat. When you hear the water rapidly boiling (you can peek now), immediately turn off the heat. Set a timer for 5 minutes and do not disturb the eggs or move the pot. (Don't peek!) Meanwhile, prepare an ice bath in a medium bowl. After 5 minutes, immediately strain and dunk the eggs in the ice bath. Let the eggs cool slightly before peeling.

Meanwhile, whisk together ½ cup **water**, ½ cup **beer** (drinker's choice), ⅓ cup **soy sauce**, ⅓ cup **mirin**, and ⅓ cup **sugar**. Put the eggs in a medium container so they will be completely submerged by the marinade (large measuring cups work well). Pour the marinade on top and refrigerate the peeled eggs overnight. Discard the marinade and store the soft-boiled eggs in the refrigerator for up to 1 week. Serve at room temperature with the ramen.

SERVE
(For 4 servings) Re-heat about 6 cups of ramen stock on the stovetop or in the microwave until piping hot. Count on 1 to 1½ cups of stock per person, depending on the size of your bowls. Cook 4 ounces of noodles per the package instructions and divide the drained noodles among serving bowls. Ladle the ramen stock on top of the noodles along with whatever toppings you are using. Nestle a sliced Beer-Cured Ajitsuke Egg in each bowl. Get slurping right away.

CONDIMENTS

Homemade condiments are seriously underrated. Add a good beer, and the average lunch or dinner sandwich becomes a mighty fine meal.

BALSAMIC NUT RELISH

We love this tangy, nutty relish spooned into canned tuna or dolloped on top of goat cheese for an instant appetizer. Kale salads share the relish love, too.

Finely chop about ½ of a medium to large **red onion**. Heat ⅓ cup of **olive oil** over medium-low heat in a high-sided saucepan. Slowly sauté the onion with a 2- to 3-inch sprig of **rosemary** until the onions are soft and barely beginning to brown. Be patient; it will take a solid 10 minutes. Turn off the heat and remove the rosemary sprig. Scrape the onions into a large bowl with two handfuls (about ½ cup) of both tender **raisins** and roughly chopped, lightly toasted **walnuts**. Pour ⅓ cup **balsamic vinegar** into the empty saucepan and simmer a few minutes, until the vinegar is reduced by roughly half. (Watch carefully, as vinegar tends to suddenly evaporate into a sticky caramel towards the end.) Immediately scrape the vinegar into the bowl, give everything a good stir, and let the relish cool completely. Stir in a generous handful of chopped **parsley** leaves and season with salt and freshly ground black pepper to taste. Makes about 1½ cups.

RED ONION STOUT MARMALADE

With a double hit of nutty, toasty notes from both stout and British-style malt vinegar, which is made from ale, these slow-cooked onions are right at home on a blue cheese burger or brioche grilled cheese (try Gruyère or a similar cheese). Use a balanced stout or porter.

Slice 3 meaty **red onions** (about 1½ pounds) into medium rings. Add enough **olive oil** to a large Dutch oven to lightly coat the bottom and turn the heat to medium. Add the onions, a leafy **thyme sprig**, and 2 or 3 chopped **sage leaves**, if you have some. Cover the pot and slowly cook the onions for a good 30 minutes (stir a few times). Stir in ¼ cup sugar, ½ cup **stout** or **porter** (leftover is fine), and ¼ cup **malt vinegar**. Turn the heat to high and rapidly boil the liquid until the onions are no longer submerged, more resting in a pool of sauce, about 15 minutes. (The sauce will still be very juicy.) Cool and season the relish with salt and freshly ground black pepper. Makes about 2 cups.

APRICOT GINGER CHUTNEY

Chutney has that IPA love-hate thing going. Lovers tend to blindly rave while doubters will hardly even try a taste. We hope this apricot version, loaded with fresh apples and ginger, will change your mind.

Choose whole, chubby dried apricots, as the pre-chopped fruits tend to be loaded with added sugar. Use the chutney as a stuffing for a rolled pork loin, add a giant spoonful or two to chicken curry, and spread it on leftover turkey sandwiches. Tweet us how it goes. @Goose_Island #chutneylove or #chutneyhmm

Finely zest 1 **orange** and squeeze all of the juice into a medium, non-reactive saucepan (like stainless steel) with high sides. Add ¼ cup (each) of **cider vinegar**, water, and packed **brown sugar**. Toss 1 chopped, unpeeled **apple** (green or yellow, maker's choice) along with about ⅓ of a chopped **red onion** into the pan with 1 smashed **garlic clove** and a 2-inch nub of grated, peeled **ginger**. Stir in 1½ cups roughly chopped **dried apricots**, ½ cup **golden raisins**, ¼ teaspoon each of **cinnamon**, **kosher salt**, and **freshly ground pepper**, and a nice pinch of **cloves**. Cover and cook the chutney over medium-low heat for about 15 minutes, stirring every so often. Let cool, discard the garlic, and season with salt and pepper to taste. Makes about 2½ cups.

HABANERO CARROT HOT SAUCE

Habanero peppers pack some serious heat. The carrots act as a faux sweet mediator in this bright orange hot sauce, so use only as many peppers as you can handle. Invite the neighbor, the one who gets really excited about jar lifters, over for a beer and canning advice. Whether you serve an Imperial IPA depends on your Scoville tolerance scale (for more on hops' effect on heat perception, see page 184).

In a large saucepan, combine ½ **onion** and 4 large **carrots** (both roughly chopped) with 4 smashed **garlic** cloves, 3 to 5 fresh **habanero chiles** (stemmed, halved, and seeded), 2 tablespoons **sugar**, 1 teaspoon **sea salt**, and a pinch each of **cinnamon**, **allspice**, and **cloves**. Stir in ⅓ cup **apple cider vinegar** and 1 cup **water**, and bring to a boil. Reduce the heat to medium-low and simmer, covered, until the vegetables are soft, 20 to 25 minutes, stirring every so often. Let cool and puree the hot sauce ingredients in a blender with 1 cup water and the juice of ½ large **lemon**. Thin the sauce with a little more water, if you'd like. Season with salt to taste. Refrigerate for up to 2 weeks, or divide the hot sauce among 4-ounce glass jars and following proper canning methods. Makes 2½ to 3 cups.

Scallops
WITH ARUGULA & BEURRE BLANC
Lemon, Butter, Capers

1 medium shallot, finely chopped

1 garlic clove, minced

1 thyme sprig

½ cup dry white wine

Juice of 1 large lemon

16 tablespoons (8 ounces; 2 sticks) cold unsalted butter, plus more for cooking

2 tablespoons heavy cream

Sea salt and white pepper

20 jumbo sea scallops (about 1½ pounds)

5 small bunches or 2 5-ounce bags (about 10 cups) baby arugula

FOR SERVING

2 tablespoons capers, lemon wedges, crusty bread

Makes 6 mains, 10 small plates

SAUCE

In a medium, non-reactive saucepan, combine the shallots, garlic, thyme, wine, and lemon juice. Bring to a boil and cook until the liquid is reduced to a few tablespoons, about 5 minutes. While the sauce is bubbling, cut the cold butter into 16 tablespoons. Reduce the heat to low (make sure the liquid is not bubbling), discard the thyme, and whisk in the cream. Add the butter one tablespoon at a time, whisking constantly. Allow each chunk of butter to fully melt before adding the next one; this should take several minutes as the sauce begins to emulsify. (You are still whisking, yes?) When all the butter has been incorporated, immediately remove the sauce from the heat and season with salt and white pepper. Use immediately, or transfer the sauce to a large bowl, cover with plastic, and keep it warm over a steaming pot of water on the stove for up to 2 hours. A thermos also works well.

SCALLOPS

Rinse the scallops and use paper towels to dry both sides well. Arrange the arugula on serving plates. Heat a large, wide saucepan over medium-high heat until very hot. Swirl a pat of butter around the pan and sear half of the scallops until golden brown on one side only, 1 to 2 minutes. Transfer the scallops to a plate.

Do the same with the remaining scallops, only this time flip them after searing one side. Return the other scallops to the pan, uncooked side facing down. Finish cooking all of the scallops, shaking the pan back and forth a few times, until medium rare, 60 to 90 seconds. They should still be soft to the touch, not springy. Season to taste with salt and white pepper.

SERVE

Arrange a few scallops on top of the arugula on each plate. Spoon several tablespoons of the warm beurre blanc sauce over each serving. Scatter the capers on top and arrange a lemon wedge alongside, and serve immediately with crusty bread. Put any remaining sauce in a bowl for the table, if you would like.

PAIRS WITH
SOFIE
HALIA
GILLIAN

We have several Certified Cicerones® working at Goose Island, so food and beer pairing conversations can get pretty enthusiastic around here. When Christina Perozzi, one of the Cicerones in charge of our education department, remembers the time she first had these warm, buttery scallops with arugula and lemon butter sauce, she lets out a lot of "mmmm" sounds. Paired with a glass of sparkling-wine-like beer, like Sofie, "It's the bomb."

Beurre blanc is not complicated, but it requires your attention. This is not the time to take selfies to prove you are actually cooking for a dinner party. The sauce will curdle if you aren't diligent about whisking constantly, or if the heat is too high. Be sure your butter is well chilled. It might be wise to buy extra butter and lemons, in case a second batch is needed. Prep the sauce an hour or two ahead, then sear the scallops when you pop the bottles of Belgian-style ale. A French chef would strain the shallots out of the sauce, but we leave them in for some urban character.

We were inspired to create this recipe when we brewed a Fulton & Wood pale ale called Devon Ave., named after the street in Chicago known for its amazing Indian food. Goose Island brewers descended upon the Patel Brothers Spice House on Devon Avenue and found the spices that would define the beer: amchoor, cardamom, and ajowan, along with chai tea from David's Tea in Canada. This beer's notes of cinnamon, tropical green mango, spicy earthiness, thyme, mint, and a waft of smoke were a revelation when paired with lamb korma takeout from Hema's Kitchen.

We love homemade versions of stews like this. Browning meat in small batches for what seems like much longer than any recipe promises it will take? Not so much. This hands-free tip—roast a large cut of meat in the oven until nicely browned, then cut it into stewing chunks—comes from a chef tight on both kitchen space and time. It works for pot roasts, too.

GOOD KORMA

Brewers are cooks. We can romanticize their work days, but they are ultimately checking off a long list of daily tasks. (Try cleaning a giant steel tank caked with blackberry seeds.) The passion comes from the story buried in those few extra spoonfuls or pounds of one ingredient or another. Maybe the cinnamon simply smelled crazy good that day. In Indian kitchens, the type and quantity of spices each cook uses to make korma are just as personal and varied.

Lamb
KORMA
Ginger, Cardamom, Star Anise

1 boneless lamb leg, roughly 5 pounds

Olive oil

Kosher salt and freshly ground pepper

2 large or 3 medium onions, roughly chopped

8 to 10 meaty garlic cloves, roughly chopped

Korma spice mix (recipe follows)

2- to 3-inch nub ginger, peeled and grated

5 tablespoons tomato paste

FOR SERVING
1 bunch chopped parsley, plenty of rice or your favorite sopping bread (naan, crusty bread)

LAMB
Preheat the oven to 475°F. Untie the roast and put it in a roasting pan or on a rimmed baking sheet. Slice partly through any meaty areas to make the lamb lay almost flat like brisket. Rub lightly with olive oil and season generously with salt and pepper. Roast, uncovered, until well browned on the outside, about 1 hour. Remove the lamb from the oven (careful, the oil is very hot) and set aside for an hour or so, until cool enough to handle.

Put the pan drippings in a jar in the fridge, and when nicely chilled, skim off and discard the fat. Cut the roast into stewing-size chunks. Leave most of the fat. (It's tasty!) Make the stew right away, or cover and refrigerate the meat overnight.

STEW
In a large Dutch oven, heat a few tablespoons of olive oil over medium heat. Sauté the onions and garlic, stirring every so often, for a good 5 minutes. Sprinkle the korma spices, ginger, and 2 teaspoons salt over the onions and give everything a good stir. Wait a minute or two, then stir in the tomato paste and 4 cups of water. Scrape any brown bits off the bottom of the pot, add the roasted meat, and bring to a boil. Reduce the heat to a simmer and add the reserved pan drippings from the roast lamb to the pot. Cook the korma, uncovered, for 2 to 2½ hours, stirring every so often. Remove the star anise (if you've used the whole ones), and season to taste with salt and pepper.

FOR THE KORMA SPICE MIX
This version uses a half dozen traditional spices with smoked paprika and cayenne standing in for Kashmiri chiles, a smoky local pepper. Try ours, or create your own spice blend. Either way, it's a handy excuse to hit the local spice shop.

Mix together: 6 to 8 whole **cardamom pods** (skins discarded, seeds smashed), 2 teaspoons **cumin seeds** (or 1 teaspoon ground), 1 teaspoon **coriander**, ½ teaspoon **cinnamon**, ⅛ teaspoon **cloves** (6 to 8 whole), 2 whole **star anise** (or ¼ teaspoon ground), 1 tablespoon **smoked paprika**, and ¼ teaspoon **cayenne pepper**, or to taste.

SERVE
Keep the korma warm on the stove until ready to serve, or let everything cool, cover, and put the stew, pot and all, in the refrigerator for a day or two. Reheat gently, stirring often to prevent scorching. Sprinkle the parsley on top and serve with rice or bread.

PAIRS WITH
GOOSE IPA
GREEN LINE
THE OGDEN

Bourbon
"BREAD PUDDING" ICE CREAM
Bourbon Pecans, Maple Bourbon Butter Sauce

3 pints good-quality vanilla ice cream like Häagen-Dazs or Ben & Jerry's

About 1½ cups Bourbon Pecans (recipe follows)

FOR SERVING

Bourbon Pecans (small handful) and Maple Bourbon Butter Sauce (recipes follow)

ICE CREAM

Roughly chop the bourbon pecans. In a large bowl, mash the ice cream and the chopped pecans together and repack the ice cream into the pint containers or another large container. Freeze for at least 3 hours, until firm, or up to 3 days. If you have a large enough freezer, you can scoop the ice cream into 6 serving bowls a few hours before you plan to serve it (this helps the ice cream stay firm when you pour the warm sauce on top).

FOR THE BOURBON PECANS

You will have more pecans than you need for the ice cream. We don't see that as a problem.

Preheat the oven to 350°F. Swipe a little butter on the bottom of a large rimmed baking sheet and line it with a Silpat mat or parchment paper. Put about 2½ cups (10 ounces) **pecan halves** in a medium heatproof bowl.

In a medium saucepan, stir together ⅓ cup **bourbon**, 4 tablespoons **unsalted butter**, ⅓ cup **brown sugar** (packed), ½ teaspoon **cinnamon**, and ½ teaspoon **kosher salt**. Heat the bourbon-butter mixture over high heat until rapidly boiling and boil until slightly thickened, 2 to 3 minutes. Immediately pour the bourbon sauce over the pecans and stir everything together with a heatproof rubber spatula. Spread the pecans on the lined baking sheet; they will clump together a little. Bake for 8 minutes. Give the pecans a good stir around the pan and bake until the sauce is really bubbling, about 5 minutes longer. Remove the nuts from the oven, let cool for 5 minutes, and then transfer them to a glass or heatproof dish. Cool completely and store in a sealed container for up to 1 week. Makes about 2½ cups.

continued on page 224

continued from page 222

FOR THE MAPLE BOURBON BUTTER SAUCE

Gently heat 1 tablespoon each of **unsalted butter** and **bourbon** with ⅓ cup **maple syrup** in a small saucepan until the butter melts. Let cool slightly before drizzling over the ice cream.

SERVE

Scoop the ice cream into serving bowls and nestle a few bourbon pecans near the side of each bowl. Drizzle a little warm Maple Bourbon Butter Sauce on top and serve the ice cream right away.

Comforting and reliable, but not out of the ballpark. At least that's how we felt about bread pudding until we tasted Paul Kahan's version at the Publican in Chicago. Ceramic terrines filled with what appeared to be the standard bread and baked custard affair appeared with Madame Rose as the finale of a multiple-course beer tasting. It was the only time everyone at the table was silent, which is no small statement to make about a table full of beer-happy international sales reps who don't often get the opportunity to gather together at our Chicago headquarters.

When we asked the chef for the recipe, it was surprisingly standard, including the note to use "whatever leftover bread you have around." And so we asked what the restaurant uses: leftover homemade sticky buns. Who has homemade sticky buns on hand to make bread pudding? Oh, right: a restaurant with a fantastic pastry chef.

Thus we moved on to ice cream, essentially a custard that has been chilled instead of baked, and folded in the flavor components of a sticky bun: caramelized pecans, cinnamon, butter, maple syrup, and a little bourbon for kicks. Store-bought vanilla ice cream even works well. Just scoop, sip (a good beer), and serve.

Barley
BROWN BUTTER SAND TARTS
Walnuts

Sand tarts are unifying, a cookie for bakers and non-bakers alike. If that sounds too political for your kitchen counter, try this: these cookies are simple to make with only a few ingredients and are also really, really good.

Don't skip the extra step of making the brown butter. It gives a toasty, nutty flavor to the cookies that works really well with the barley flour. Speaking of, the flour isn't here for the obvious beer ingredient parallels, though sure, you could work that into your tasting-party introduction. The flour lends more of that intangible quality, like whatever ingredient is in that *really* good beer at a blind tasting that no one can pinpoint. Scout out a bag of the flour, which you will also want for the waffles (page 203), and you're ready to roll.

16 tablespoons (8 ounces; 2 sticks) unsalted butter

1 teaspoon vanilla extract

1 cup powdered sugar, plus more for dusting

1 cup all-purpose flour

1⅓ cups barley flour

¾ teaspoon kosher salt

About 32 walnut halves or pieces

BROWN BUTTER

In a high-sided saucepan, bring the butter to a low boil until it foams. Don't fire up the heat too much, or the butter may bubble over, and use a heatproof rubber spatula to scrape the bottom of the pan every so often. After 4 to 5 minutes, you should see toasty brown flecks on the bottom of the pan. Scrape the toasted butter and all of the brown bits into a large, heatproof mixing bowl. Let the butter cool for a few minutes, or refrigerate for up to 3 days until you are ready to bake. Re-melt the butter on the stovetop or in the microwave.

COOKIES

Preheat the oven to 350°F. Line two baking sheets with a Silpat mat or parchment paper. Use a whisk to mix together the melted butter, vanilla extract, and powdered sugar until most of the lumps are gone. There's no need to go crazy; a few sugar lumps are fine. Now, switch to a spoon and stir in both flours and the salt, then mix with your hands so the dough is nicely combined.

Use a measuring spoon to scoop out roughly 32 tablespoon-size pieces of dough and roughly shape each piece into a chubby disc about 1½ inches in diameter. Place half of the dough rounds an inch or two apart on each baking sheet and lightly press a walnut half into each. Bake the cookies until set and just beginning to brown on the bottom, 15 to 16 minutes, flipping the baking pans from the top to the bottom rack and front to back halfway through baking. Cool the cookies completely on the baking sheets. Before serving, sift as much powdered sugar over the cookies as you'd like.

PAIRS WITH
HONKERS
WINTER ALE
FESTIVITY ALE

GOOSE ISLAND
BEER COMPANY

is a pioneer of the craft brewing movement. This brewery is built on a culture of immense curiosity and relentless exploration. The brewers are empowered to challenge the established conventions of brewing and aging beer, and constantly experiment with ingredients and process. First and foremost, we are beer lovers."

—Goose Island Beer Company

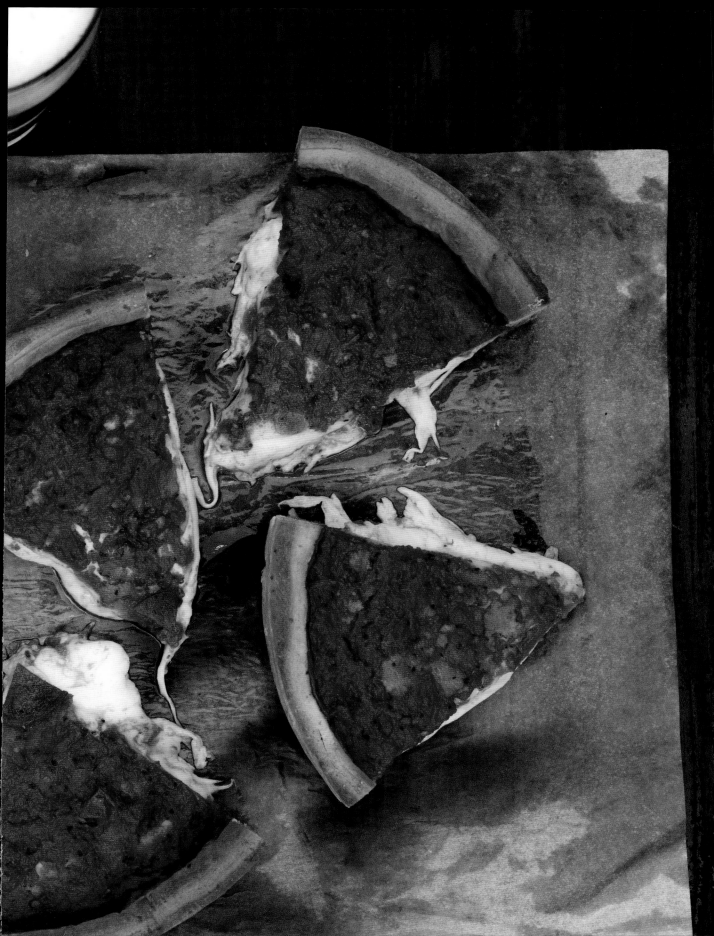

ACKNOWLEDGMENTS

Who knew it would require moving a few foudres to get beer people to sit down and produce a beer book that covered so many variables? First and foremost, we wouldn't have a book or a company without the invention and bravery of founder John Hall and founding brewmaster Greg Hall, as as well as the hard work and dedication of our brewers. A big round of applause to our brewmaster, Jared Jankowski, and his entire brewing team.

We were lucky to start off with an incredible food team, including food photographer Staci Valentine and stylists Vivian Lui and Sienna DeGovia. For recipes, we pried the Japanese soup out of ramen-obsessed brewer Ryan Brei and scored the bulgogi tacos from staffer Jesse Valenciana, our resident cookbook expert. Paul Kahan of the Publican and One Off Hospitality Group has been indispensable at Goose in so many roles; we might not cook as well as he does, but we certainly get plenty of recipe inspiration, including the bread pudding here. The remaining recipes we developed with Jenn Garbee, who took inspiration from Goose brewers and staffers—not exactly the types to be shy about their food opinions.

Resident Goose Island photographer Ken Hunnemeder was the cameraman behind most of the Goose Island photos throughout the book, along with Mike Erickson and Ryan Grillaert. Thank you all for making the book look and feel so rad.

Everyone at Lentini Design & Marketing deserves a standing applause for making the book so approachable and beer-friendly visually, especially Art Director Hilary Lentini and Lead Designer Leanna Hanson for all the creativity, and Michelle McAllister for helping us stick to the schedule.

Amy Inouye of Future Studio also provided great cover inspiration. We can't thank you enough for the beautiful and brilliant work.

WE WOULDN'T HAVE A BOOK *or a company without the invention and bravery of founder John Hall and founding brewmaster Greg Hall."*

We all know the real brewing labor happens behind the scenes, long before the labels are designed and the seasonal release events are planned. Publisher Colleen Dunn Bates and the staff at Prospect Park Books offered more guidance and patience (last call for another round!) than we deserved. Thanks to copy editor Lori Martinsek and longtime Clybourn brewer-turned-factchecker Jon Naghski, as well as so many of the staff at Goose Island: Ken Stout, T.J. Annerino, Mara Melamed, Megan Lagesse, and Jennifer Ohrn. Oh, and we're grateful to Cara Condon for her infallible—and stinky—cheese knowledge.

Thank you again to Jenn Garbee for helping to research and write the whole shebang, a project that grew as the book expanded—even we didn't realize what was lurking in the depths of those Bourbon County Brand Stout barrels of old. And finally, a big thanks to Christina Perozzi for coming up with the idea to write this book, editing it with a beer educator's eyes, and making the project a reality every step of the way.

— Goose Island Beer Company

INDEX

1516, 49, 135,136, 185, 188, 192

2-Row, 59, 87, 88,92, 96, 99, 107, 108, 111, 115, 124, 127, 128, 131, 139, 149

3-30-300 rule, 165

312 Urban Wheat, 31, 36, 88, 151, 153, 155, 159, 166, 169, 173, 176, 182, 205, 213

4 Hands Brewing Company, 71

Abbaye Notre-Dame d'Orval, 98

ABV, 72, 83

acetaldehyde, 75

aftertaste, 159, 160, 162

age, 26, 50, 53, 78, 79, 100, 103, 121, 127, 132, 140, 143, 165, 166, 169

aging, barrel, 24, 43, 50, 53, 63, 76, 79, 115, 131, 132, 139, 143, 189

aging process, 66, 76, 78, 79, 116, 131, 165

alcohol content, 59, 60, 72, 76, 83, 84, 160, 165, 184, 193

ale

American pale, 39, 91

Belgian-style, 76, 96, 100, 102, 103, 184, 194

Brewery Yard Stock, 143

Casimir, 136

cask-conditioned, 153

classic, 84

cream, 135

definition of, 58

farmhouse, 96, 99, 108, 111

Goose Winter, 182

Green Line Pale, 36, 91, 151, 166, 173, 176, 178, 180, 183, 192, 212, 221

Honkers, 7, 12, 14, 20, 21, 92, 95, 151, 166, 169, 173, 176, 178, 180, 182, 190, 192-194, 198, 208, 225

Orval, 98-99

pale, 39, 59, 81, 84, 87, 88, 91, 92, 98, 112, 139, 143, 149-151, 155, 156, 173, 180, 184, 220

Pilgrim Yeast House, 112, 115

Polish-style smoked wheat, 136

Scotch, 139

sour, 102, 147, 159

sparkling, 136

Trappist-style, 39, 98-99, 156

wheat, 73, 88, 89, 135, 136, 155, 159

wild, 71, 102

Wild Red, 140

winter, 150, 151, 155, 166, 178, 182, 192-194

Amarillo hops, 36, 96, 108

American pale ale, 39, 91

American Society of Brewing Chemists, 150

ancho chiles, 208

Angel's Share, 78, 79

Anheuser-Busch InBev (ABI), 32

annual release calendar, 102

apple, 127, 156, 165, 181, 189, 190, 205, 217

apple cider, 205, 217

Apricot Ginger Chutney, 217

aromas 60, 66, 74, 75

ASBC, 150

Atkins, Ed, 35

Australian-style sparkling ale, 136

avocado, 210, 211

Balsamic Nut Relish, 217

Bamforth, Charles, 179

barley, 57, 59, 60, 74, 88, 92, 124, 127, 128, 131, 136, 139, 185, 202, 203, 224, 225

Barley Brown Butter Sand Tarts, 224

barley flour, 202, 203, 224, 225

barley malt, 88

barley, roasted, 59, 60, 92, 124, 127, 128

barleywine, 26, 53, 116, 121, 131, 132, 166, 173, 176, 192

barrel aging, 24, 43, 50, 53, 63, 65, 76, 79, 115, 131, 132, 139-140, 143, 199

Barrel Warehouse, 26, 31, 32, 50, 79, 132

Barrel-Aged Blonde Doppelbock, 139

Barrel-Aged Scotch Ale, 139

Barrelhouse Series, 139

barrels

bourbon, 50, 132, 139

Bourbon County Brand Rare, 53, 116, 121

Knob Creek, 50, 121

layers in, 79

oak neutral wine, 78, 79, 107, 108,
        111, 112, 115
    preparation, 78
    rye whiskey, 53, 77, 79, 128, 132
    white oak, 53, 121, 132
    wine, 46, 50, 53, 79, 100, 103, 107,
        108, 111, 112, 115, 149
    wood, 28, 79, 102, 116
Bartender Haze, 150
base malts, 59
Bavarian Hefeweizen, 71
Bavarian Kellerbier, 136
Bavarian weiss, 49, 135, 156
Bavarian wheat yeast, 71
Bavarian-style Rauch-Kellerbier,
    49, 189
Bee Squad, 136, 192, 194
Beef Marinade, 208
Beer Advocate, 107, 108, 111, 112, 132
beer cocktails, 204
beer color, 59, 149-151
beer pairing, 18, 190, 219
Beer Purity Law, 49
beer tasting, 147, 160, 223
Beer Tasting Record, 162, 163
Beer Tasting Wheel, 162
Beer-Cured Ajitsuke Eggs, 212
Belgian "Orval" Clone, 107
Belgian Dubbel, 72
Belgian Framboise, 107
Belgian Lambics, 102

Belgian-style ales, 76, 96, 100, 102,
    103, 184, 194
Belgian-style farmhouse ale, 96,
    108, 111
Belgian-style tripel, 19
Belgian-style Witbier, 150
Berliner Weisse, 49

Bière de miele, 136
bitter (beer), 81, 87, 88, 91, 92, 164,
    173, 182, 197
bitter (flavor), 65, 66, 183
bittering, 39, 66, 68, 83, 92
Black Friday, 23, 118, 119, 124, 127,
    128, 131

Blancquaert-Merck, Rosa, 114

Blonde Doppelbock, 135, 139

bottle conditioning, 153

bottling, 28, 31, 79, 84, 87, 88, 91, 92, 96, 103, 107, 108, 111, 112, 115, 124, 127, 128, 131, 166

bourbon, 26, 50, 116, 117, 119, 125, 222

Bourbon "Bread Pudding" Ice Cream, 222

bourbon barrel aging, 50, 132, 139

bourbon barrel-aged beer, 26, 27, 50, 79, 116, 117, 131, 132, 139

Bourbon County Brand Stouts
Backyard Rye, 77, 79
Barleywine, 53, 116, 121, 131
Bramble Rye, 193
Coffee Stout, 28, 116, 121, 127, 128, 191, 193
flavor diversity in, 193
Northwoods, 121
Proprietor's Blend, 26, 46, 79, 116, 121, 128, 166, 193
Rare, 53, 116, 121, 132
Rare Barleywine, 53, 132
Rare barrels, 53, 116, 121
Regal Rye, 53, 132
Reserve, 50, 116, 121
Reserve Barleywine, 116, 121
Single Vintage, 132
Special Releases, 116
Stout, 23, 24, 26-27, 32, 36, 49 50, 53, 65, 66, 77, 78-79, 116, 118, 124, 150, 160-61, 176-77, 182, 189, 191

Bourbon County series, 26, 66, 118, 120-23, 128, 132, 153, 159, 166, 192-94

Bourbon Pecans, 222

Brasserie Series, 53, 79

Brei, Ryan, 215

Brett beers, 71

Brett Claussennii yeast, 143

Brettanomyces, 71, 99, 100, 102, 107, 108, 111, 112, 115, 156

Brewer's Waffles, 203

Brewery Yard Stock Ale, 143

brewhouses, 72

brewing process, 7, 49-50, 59, 60, 63, 65, 66, 68, 72, 74, 76, 90, 96, 102, 104, 149, 150

Brooklyn Brewery, 115

Brown Butter Sand Tarts, 225

Brynildson, Matt, 22, 25, 46, 85

Bulgogi Breakfast Tacos, 206

Burton upon Trent, 143

C.A.L.M. Radler, 49, 135, 173, 180, 204, 205, 211

Campaign for Real Ale, 153

CAMRA, 153

caramelization, 60

carbon dioxide, 63, 71, 72, 150, 165, 172

carbonation, 59, 63, 72, 88, 92, 149, 150, 160, 165, 169, 173, 176, 178

Cascade hops, 36, 84, 88

Casimir ale, 136

cask-conditioned, 72, 153

Castelvetrano olives 212, 213

caviar, 198

cellarman, 50, 71, 135

Centennial hops, 36, 84

Century of Progress Exhibition, 87

chalice, 96, 99, 103, 107, 108, 111, 112, 115, 172, 173, 205

Champagne yeast, 102, 110, 111

Chance the Rapper, 143

Chateau Blanc, 53

Chateau Noir, 53

cheese, 86, 176, 180-182, 185, 186, 190, 192, 202, 217

cheese varieties, pairing with beer, 180, 182

Cherry-Orange Compote, 202, 203

Chicago Barrel Warehouse, 50

Chicago Beer Society, 23

Chicago Fire, 87

Chicago Land Company, 18

Chicago terroir, 78

Chicago's West Side, 50

Chicken Shio Ramen, 212

Chill Haze, 150

chocolate, 21, 59, 60, 76, 78, 79, 115, 116, 124, 127, 128, 131, 151, 159, 179, 183, 194

chutney, 217

Chris Knight Creation, 28

Cicerone, 178

Cider, Matilda Spiked, 205

citrus fruits, 210-211

clarity, 149, 150, 160, 162, 165, 169

Clybourn, 7, 12, 14, 16-18, 21-24, 28, 88, 111, 119, 139

Clybourn Brewpub, 16, 24, 28, 88, 111

Clybourn, Archibald, 12, 16

cocktails, 24, 172, 204, 205

coffee, 16, 26, 28, 49, 60, 66, 72, 76, 78, 79, 116, 118, 121, 127, 149, 151, 159, 161, 166, 173, 190-194, 202

Coir Fiber, 40

color wheel, 60

Columbus, 127, 128

Condiments, 217

cookies, 225

Cooper Project, 50, 76, 79, 138, 139

Cornell, Martyn, 143

cream ale, 135

Cthulhu, 31

cucumber, 135, 213

Dark Traveler, 135, 136

Davis, Brian, 136

debittered black malts, 59

Devil's Cut, 78, 79

Devon Ave., 220

diacetyl, 74

dimethyl sulfide, 74

DMS, 74

Domaine de canton, 205

doppelbock, 49, 135, 139, 156

dry hopping, 68

dubbels, 72, 99

Dunkelroggenweizenbock, 135

East Kent Golding, 139

eggs, 75, 176, 189, 203, 206, 212

Elijah Craig, 31

Elk Mountain, 35, 36, 40, 66, 84, 87

English hops, 39

English-style bitter (ESB), 81, 92, 164, 182

esters, 71, 72, 73, 153

Experimental beers, 36, 49, 143

Extra-Special Bitter, 164

farmhouse ales, 96, 99, 173, 178, 194

Fassinator, 135, 136, 192, 194

fermentation, 28, 31, 53, 57-59, 63, 68,
    72, 74, 75, 100, 102, 103, 115, 140,
    153, 189

fermentation, primary, 53, 100,
    103, 140

fermentation, secondary, 53, 102, 103,
    115, 153

fermenters, 28

Fest Bier, 166, 172, 178, 182, 193, 194

Festival of Wood and Barrel Aged
    Beer, 26

Festivity Ale, 173, 231

filtration, 58, 63, 149

Firestone Walker Brewing, 22, 25, 85

First Wort Hopping, 68

flank steak, 206

flavors, off, 72, 75

Fleur de Saison 204

flour tortillas, 208, 209

foie gras, 189, 199

Foudre Project, 53, 140

foudres, 50, 53, 140

Four Star Pils, 14, 31, 36, 86, 87, 151,
    160, 166, 169, 173, 176, 178, 180,
    199, 212

freezing point, 165

Fremont Brewing, 46

Fried Eggs, 208

fuggle hops, 39

Fulton & Wood beers, 46

Fulton & Wood Method, 49

Fulton Street Brewery, 18, 28, 31, 32,
    45, 46, 50, 73, 88, 91, 104

Fulton Street Taproom, 28, 29, 153

fusel, 74, 75

German Hüll Melon hops, 99

Gillian, 53, 102, 104, 110, 111, 151, 166,
    173, 189, 192, 194, 199, 218

ginger, 39, 76, 204-208, 211, 214, 215,
    217, 221

glassware, 103, 172, 173

glassware, shapes, 172

glassware, varieties
    chalice, 96, 99, 103, 107, 108, 111,
        112, 115, 172, 173, 213
    Imperial Stout, 124, 127, 128,
        131, 172
    nonic pint, 84, 88, 91, 92, 172, 173
    pilsner, 87, 172, 173
    pint glass, 172, 173
    stange, 172, 173
    stein, 172, 173
    stemmed chalice, 103
    vintage, 96, 99, 193, 197, 198,
        111, 112, 115, 172, 173, 213
    Weizen (Weissbier) , 88, 173

Golden Goose Pilsner, 14, 21

Goose Island Barrel Warehouse, 50

Goose Island Brewmaster, 23, 24, 86,
    154, 161

Goose Island Innovation Manager, 46

Goose Island MBA, 23

Goose Island Wrigleyville, 31

Goose Oktoberfest, 151

Goose Winter Ale, 182

Goose Wrigleyville BBQ Chips, 32

grains, 57, 59, 60, 63, 74, 135, 149, 150

grapefruit, 212

gravlax, 209

Great American Beer Festival
    (GABF), 26, 84, 85, 88, 96, 99, 154

Great Chicago Fire, 87

Green Line train, 91

Green Line Pale Ale, 36, 91, 151, 166,
    173, 176, 178, 180, 183, 192, 212,
    221

Greenwood, Zach, 128

grissette, 135

gruit, 39

Habanero Carrot Hot Sauce, 217

Hagen Fish Market, 136

Halia, 53, 102, 104, 108, 151, 166, 173,
    182, 189, 192, 194, 213, 218

Hall, Greg, 23-26, 86, 87, 116, 154, 161

Hall, John, 7, 11-17, 32, 45, 49, 87, 92,
    93, 96

Hall, John J., 45, 73, 89

Hallertau hops, 35, 36, 87

haze, 150

head, 23, 28, 32, 72, 73, 77, 81, 90, 92,
    103, 135, 149, 150, 170, 172, 173

heat effects, 165

Heaven Hill Distilleries, 121, 132

Helles-style lager, 143

Herb-Cured Gravlax, 209

herbs / spices, 57, 76, 103, 179

Honkers Ale, 7, 12, 14, 20, 21, 92, 93,
    151, 166, 169, 173, 176, 178, 180,
    182, 190, 192-194, 196, 206, 225

hops, 34-41, 57, 60, 65-69, 150

    Continental, 39

    dry, 68

    Elk Mountain, 36

    English, 39

    haze, 150

    history, 39

    New World, 39

    trivia, 40

    twine, 40

    varieties, 36

hot sauce, 217

Humulus lupulus, 65, 66

IBU, 65, 85

ice cream, 182, 190-192, 202, 222-223

Illinois (beer) 151, 166, 173, 176,
    178, 183

India Pale Ale *(see also: IPA)*, 81, 84,
    85, 155

ingredients, adjunct, 57, 66, 72, 76

Initial Vintage Release, 102

Innovation Team, 46, 99

Intelligentsia, 28, 127

intensity, 76, 79, 149, 194

IPAs 81, 84, 85, 155

    double, 143, 195

Goose 36, 46, 65, 66, 84, 85, 151, 159,
    160, 166, 173, 176-178, 182, 183,
    190, 192, 199, 205

Imperial, 49, 183, 184, 201, 217

Pimm's 205

West Coast, 84

isomerization, 65

James Beard Foundation Awards, 99

Jankoski, Jared, 86

Jim Beam, 26, 50, 116

Johnston, Will, 71

Juliet, 46, 53, 102, 104, 112, 151, 166,
    173, 177, 189, 192, 194

Kahan, Paul, 99, 224

Karamoor Estate Wines, 53

Karras, Jason, 136

Kendall College, 18, 45

kilning/roasting, 59

Knight, Chris, 28

Knob Creek, 50, 121

Kobe beef, 207

Kölsch, 73, 143, 147, 150, 151, 155,
    166, 172, 173, 176, 180, 182,
    192, 211

Kombu, 186, 187, 214

Korder, Tom, 49

Kosmal, Emily, 64, 128

lacing test, 171

Laffler, John, 13

lager, 7, 14, 20, 21, 58, 81, 87, 135, 136,
    143, 173
    American light, 81
    definition of, 58
    Helles-style, 143
    Lincoln Park, 7, 14, 20, 21
    Preseason, 173

Lamb Korma, 147, 220, 221

lambic cultures, 115

lautering, 63

Liefmans brewery, 114

Lilith, 49, 189

Lincoln Park Lager, 7, 14, 20, 21

Lincoln, Matt, 46

Lloyd Wright, Frank, 156

Lolita, 53, 102, 104, 106, 107, 149, 151,
    159, 166, 173, 189, 192, 194

Lovibond, 150

lupulin glands, 66

Madame Rose, 46, 53, 102, 104, 114,
    115, 151, 160, 166, 173, 182, 189,
    192, 194, 203, 218, 223

Maillard Reaction, 60

malt
    aromatics, 60
    barley 88
    base, 59
    basics, 59-60
    flavor, 60, 135, 193
    green, 59
    process, 59-60
    rye, 136
malting, 59, 63
malts, 59, 60
Maple Bourbon Butter Sauce, 228
maple syrup, 76, 128, 192, 193, 202, 203, 222, 223
marmalade, 217
mascarpone, 203
mash tuns, 28
Master of Beer Appreciation, 21, 23
Matilda, 71, 73, 79, 99, 102, 103, 151, 153, 156, 160, 166, 173, 182, 184, 192, 194, 198, 205
Matilda Apple Toddy, 205
Matilda Spiked Cider, 205
maturation, 58, 63
Millenium hops, 36
Mount Hood hops, 36
Munich, 35, 45, 59, 112, 127, 128, 131, 136, 139
Munich Dunkel, 136
mushrooms, shiitake, 220
My Shout, 135, 136
Naghski, Jon, 23

National Rye Variant, 121
Natural Villain, 143, 173
New World hops, 39, 88
nitrogenated beers, 72, 150
No Collar, 143
Noble hops, 39
Noe, Booker, 26, 50, 116, 121
Nugget hops, 36
oak foudres, 53, 140
oak neutral wine barrels, 78, 79, 107, 108, 111, 112, 115
Off Color Brewing, 13
Ogden, 18, 19, 178, 192, 221
Ogden Island, 18
Ogden, William, 18
Ohrn, Jennifer, 29
Oktoberfest, 151, 192
Old World hops, 39
Oliver, Garrett, 115
orange juice, 96, 203, 205
Orval, 98, 99, 107
Orval Foundation, 98
Oud Bruin, 114, 115, 140
oxidation, 74, 75, 165
packaging, 28, 63, 165
Pattison, Ron, 143
pear sour, 135
Penrose Brewing, 49
Perennial, 46
Petite Matilda, 99
Petite Orval, 99
phenols, 72, 75, 173

Pilgrim Yeast House Ale, 112, 115
Pilot Brewery, 28, 31, 36, 46, 49, 76
pils, 14, 31, 36, 86, 87, 89, 139, 151, 160, 166, 169, 173, 176, 178, 180, 199, 208, 214
Pilsen-style beer, 73
pilsner, 13, 14, 21, 59, 65, 66, 72, 81, 86, 87, 89, 108, 111, 150, 159, 172, 173, 178, 180, 214
pilsner
    American-style, 87
    Four Star Pils, 31, 173
    glass, 87, 172, 173
    Golden Goose, 14, 21
Pimm's IPA, 204
pistachios, 212, 213
Pitchfork Music Festival, 46, 143
Pitchfork Music Festival
    Collaboration Beers, 143
Polish Lublin hops, 136
Polish-style smoked wheat ale, 136
porter
    Baltic, 139
    Barrel-Aged, 139
    Holiday 139
    Old Clybourn, 14, 21, 139
Porter, Brett, 32, 71, 73, 77, 90, 128
Preseason Lager, 173
preservative, 65, 66, 84
Prohibition, 13, 40
Proprietor's Blend, 26, 46, 79, 116, 121, 128, 166, 193

Pub Chips, 31

Publican, 223

Pulaski, Casimir 136

Quick Pickled Red Onions, 208

rack, 81, 103, 225

radler, 49, 135, 173, 180, 192, 204,
206, 211

ramen, 212

rasselbock, 49, 135, 156, 173,
122, 193

ratings in tastings, 83

Red Chile-Tomatillo Salsa, 208

Red Onion Stout Marmalade, 217

Reinheitsgebot, 136

Reisch, Patrick, 135

Relish, 217

richness / mouthfeel, 59, 60

Riesling grape juice, 53

Rodriguez, Diana "Di", 128

roggenbier, 49, 135, 156

rolled oats, 203

Roselarre, 115

rye malt, 136

rye whiskey barrels, 53, 77, 79,
128, 132

Saaz hops, 36, 99, 107

Saccharomyces cerevisiae, 71

saison yeast, 71

Saisons, 96, 194

salt test, 171

sanitization, 75

scallops, 86, 189, 218, 219

Scallops with Arugula & Beurre
Blanc, 218

Scotch Ale, 139

Seasonal, 36, 49, 102, 205

Senne River Valley, 102

serving, 13, 21, 103, 147, 164, 165, 169,
173, 203, 205, 208, 211-214, 218,
221, 222, 225

serving temperature, 165, 169

session, 88, 92-94, 99

sessionable, 12, 14, 87, 91, 92, 143

shandys, 204

sheeting (water) test, 171

Shio Broth, 212

Shred the Gnar, 49

Sicilian-Style Citrus Salad, 211

Siebel Institute of Technology,
18, 45

Siegel, Mike, 50, 128, 136, 143

skunked, 75, 165

smoking, 136, 149

snifter, 103, 124, 127, 128, 131,
172, 173

Sofie, 96, 211. 203, 204, 209,
211, 219

Sofie-Mosa, 96, 203, 204

Sorachi Ace hops 36

sours
ale, 102, 115, 147, 159
Brett, 71
pear, 135
Sour Sisters, 102-104

South Bend, Indiana, 26

sparging, 63, 74

Spaten-Franziskaner-Bräu, 135

SRM, 150, 151

St. Germain, 205

stale beer, 165

Standard Reference Method
(SRM), 150

stange, 172, 173

steak, 206

steelhead trout fillet, 209

steeping process, 65, 66

stein, 172, 173

stemmed chalice, 103

storage temperature, 81, 165

Stout, Ken, 7

stouts
barrel-aged, 116, 160, 194
Bourbon County Brand, 23, 24,
26, 28, 32, 36, 49, 50, 53, 65, 66,
76, 78, 79, 102, 116, 118, 119,
121, 124, 127, 128, 131, 132,
136, 139, 150, 151, 153, 154, 159,
160, 165, 166, 169, 173, 176,
177, 182, 189-194
Honest, 14, 20, 21
Imperial, 26, 53, 124, 127, 128,
131, 154, 172, 173
Irish, 135, 193
Proprietor's Bourbon County
Brand, 128
Russian Imperial, 154, 173

strobiles, 66

sugars, residual, 58, 60, 65, 75

sulfur, 75, 178

Summertime Kölsch, 151, 155, 166, 173, 176, 180, 172, 192, 211

SVE, 143

sweeteners, 76

tacos, 206

tannins, 60, 65, 74, 104, 107, 111, 112, 182, 184, 197

tasselbock, 135

tasting record, 162, 163

tasting wheel, 162

tea, black, 205

Thirst Fursday, 23

tomatillos, 208, 209

toro (tuna), 207

torrified wheat, 88, 108, 111

tortillas, flour, 208, 209

Trappist-style ale, 39, 98-99, 156

tripels, 19, 99, 178

triple crème, 182

trout, 209

truffles, 196

Twin Peaks, 143

umami, 136, 153, 177, 183, 185-189, 199, 214

unfiltered beer, 73, 88, 149, 153

Union Park, 143

Urban Ginger C.A.L.M. Daiquiri, 205

Valenciana, Jesse, 215

vegetables, 76, 180, 185, 189, 217

vertical tasting, 103

Vintage Appeal, 103

Virtue Cider Company, 23, 24, 154, 161

von Etten, Sharon, 143

waffles, 203

walnuts, 151, 217, 224

water, 13, 32, 57-59, 63, 65, 66, 72-75, 92, 111, 128, 136, 160, 171, 172, 179, 203, 208, 211, 212, 214, 217, 218, 221 water, hard and soft 73

water sheeting test, 171

Wee Heavy, 139

Weihenstephan, 135, 156

whiskey, 50, 53, 77, 79, 132, 203

wild ales, 71, 102

Wild Red Ale, 140

Wild Yeast Fermentation Room,
    28, 31

Willamette hops 36

wine barrel-aging, 50, 53, 63, 79, 140

wine barrels, 46, 50, 53, 79, 100, 103,
    107, 108, 111, 112, 115, 149

wine crushers/destemmers, 104

Wine-Like Qualities, 103

Winter Ale, 150, 151, 155, 166, 178,
    182, 192-194

wood barrels, 28, 79, 102, 116

World Beer Cup Awards, 99

World Brewing Academy, 45

World Series, 31

World's Columbian Exposition 87

wort, 59, 60, 63, 65, 68, 69, 74, 76, 150

Wrigley Field, 31

Wymore, Phil, 46

Yakima Valley, 40

yeast

    autolysis, 75

    Bavarian wheat, 71

    Brett Claussennii, 143

    cannibalism, 75

    champagne, 102, 110, 111

    Roselarre, 115

    saison, 71

    strains, 49, 71, 74, 115

Zythophile, 143